"These authors have uncovered an exceptionally sig~
approach to seizing the opportunity between pastors ~
is in contrast to the typical approach of merel~
next visionary leader to come to the rescu~
with caring candor about the importa~
renewal, redesign, redefinition, and rea
healthy and focused church ready for a ι
very helpful resource." — *Dr. Paul E. Mag.*   *.eritus,*
Briercrest College and Seminary

"*Between Pastors* is a much needed handbook for church leaders —
especially those helping a congregation navigate closure on the
past and prepare for the successful ministry of the next pastor. I
have known Cam Taylor for over twenty years, and this book
reflects his "shepherd's heart." Having served as a transitional
pastor in several churches, I only wish I had had this book sooner.
I highly recommend it!" — *Rev. Herb Neufeld, Transitional Pastor
with the Mennonite Brethren Church*

"One of my most challenging and rewarding ministries was to
serve a church in transition between lead pastors. Churches with
the right transitional leader can take steps so the new lead pastor
can jump into a healthier church that already has some forward
momentum. I only wish I had been exposed to this material
sooner in my ministry!" — *Dr. Randy Wollf, Assistant Professor of
Practical Theology and Leadership Studies at ACTS Seminaries of
Trinity Western University*

"*Between Pastors* is a great 'how to' book for anyone working through a pastoral transition. The book is written by two experienced colleagues who put into practical terms a proven process. This book is a must read!" — *Dr. Gerry Kraft, Founding Executive Director of Outreach Canada*

"*Between Pastors* is a treasure for every person involved in pastoral transitions. The book provides an ideal balance between strategic analysis and Spirit-led leadership — all moving toward increased congregational health and vitality. Though focused on transitions, it reflects such a mature view of congregational life that any church leader could benefit from its insights, at any point in the life of a congregation. I wish this had been available when I was coaching churches...between pastors." — *Dr. Gary Walsh, Former Executive Director of the Evangelical Fellowship of Canada*

"Cam Taylor and Alan Simpson have captured the essence of transitional ministry in a practical, usable, and understandable format. This book wonderfully shares a rich heritage of learning and experience gained through working with numerous churches. Useful for both the layperson and the transitional pastor, it offers many resources for a congregation experiencing a season of change. What takes this book from good to great is the ongoing emphasis on transition as an opportunity for spiritual formation." — *Rev. Gerry Teichrob, Director of Pathways Forward Transitional Ministry Consulting*

BETWEEN PASTORS

Seizing the Opportunity

By Cam Taylor
with
Alan Simpson

Between Pastors
Copyright © 2014 by Outreach Canada Ministries

Copyeditor: James R. Coggins
Cover Design: Ryan Toyota

Published in Canada by Outreach Canada Ministries
ISBN 978-0-9694564-9-0

Dedicated to Doug Harris

On whose shoulders this ministry is built and continues to grow.

About the Authors

Cam Taylor is the Director of the Transitional Leadership Ministries (TLM) of Outreach Canada and is actively involved in coaching and training leaders. He has over 21 years of pastoral experience and has worked with congregations in transition as a coach and leader. He has an MDiv from Western Evangelical Seminary and is an Associate Certified Coach (ACC) with the International Coach Federation (ICF).

Alan Simpson is the previous Director of TLM and has been involved in transitional leadership and training transitional leaders for the past ten years. He is a facilitator of difficult conversations, a conflict coach, and a mediator for individuals and groups. His education includes a Bachelor of Theology, an MA in Conflict Management, and a Certificate in Third-Party Mediation Intervention. He has 30 years of experience in pastoring, coaching, and training adults, families, and organizations. Alan is a skills coach and facilitative instructor for the Justice Institute of BC and has his own mediation and facilitation practice (alansimpson.ca).

Contents

How to Use This Book

T his book is a road map for those looking for help and direction when working with a congregation in pastoral transition. It is designed for the uninformed reader as well as the experienced practitioner. Practical and informative, it includes stories, illustrations, metaphors, graphs, and images intended to help bring the principles and concepts to life.

You can read this book from start to finish or use it as a reference book. You may want to read the book through quickly the first time and then, on the second reading, slow down and reflect on the questions at the end of each chapter. To better understand the way we define the words and terms we will be using throughout the book, see Appendix A.

One caution: you will not, through reading this book, miraculously acquire the skills necessary to do the work of transitional ministry. Skills such as leading, coaching, facilitating, leading change, managing conflict, and shepherding are ultimately learned in the arena of action and not from a book. This book will provide a framework for how to think about leadership in the context of intentional interim ministry and give guidance on how to facilitate the transition that takes place in a congregation when it is between pastors.

Here are some further details about how *Between Pastors* is designed in order to help make your reading more valuable:

Audience. This book is written for church leaders responsible for facilitating or supervising congregational ministry during the time between pastors. You may be a seasoned pastor looking to make transitional ministry your focus, an experienced transitional leader in the trenches, a denominational leader supervising churches in transition, or a member of a church board desiring to know how to be more effective in your congregation's transition.

You can read this book as a beginner eager to learn the nuts and bolts of intentional interim ministry or as an experienced practitioner and coach needing to be reminded of the basics.

Hyperlinks. *Between Pastors* contains several hyperlinks you can click if you are reading the e-book version. These same links can be found at www.betweenpastors.com if you are reading the print version of this book. On the website, we also provide tools and templates to support you in the work of intentional interim ministry.

Discussion Questions. At the end of each chapter, we offer discussion questions to assist with your personal and group reflection and interaction. The questions give you an opportunity to process the concepts and make a connection with your situation, experience, and current thinking. The more you reflect and engage with the material, the more you will receive from it. We encourage you to convey your learning to another person as soon as possible. This will assist in the transference from thinking to learning and increase retention.

Training. The ideas and material shared in this book are also presented in a workshop designed for those involved in this ministry. If you are serious about using these concepts and ideas in practice, check out www.betweenpastors.com for training dates. We are also open to an invitation to come and conduct a training event in your area.

Now, let's get started on your transitional ministry journey.

Acknowledgements

We want to say thank you to several people who helped with the creation of *Between Pastors*. First, there are Doug Harris and Gerry Kraft of Outreach Canada, whose vision and hard work gave birth to this ministry. Then there are the people who contributed their time, expertise, and passion in generous and valuable ways over the years as part of the training and support team: Craig Kraft, Bob Rose, John Radford, Larry Nelson, Robert Kuhn, Darrin Hotte, Gerry Teichrob, Olu Peters, Hugh Fraser, Eugene Neudorf, Dianne Boyle, Lisa Zastre, Heather Kraft, Phil Cox, and Maggie Cox.

A special thanks to all those who contributed stories and examples to the book: Abe Funk, Dennis Camplin, Dennis Scott, Dave Jackson, Bruce Sticklee, Gerry Teichrob, and Andrew Hurrell. We also say thanks to those who helped get this book ready for publication: James R. Coggins, our copyeditor; Ryan Toyota, our cover designer; Phil Cox, who helped with technical and graphical support; and Joan Taylor, who provided proofreading support. We also say thanks to the many others who shared ideas, feedback, and encouragement all along the way.

Introduction: A Cautionary Tale

O nce upon a time, in a kingdom not so far away…
Life wasn't perfect, but everyone was pretty comfortable with how things were.

The king was a good leader. He looked out for the interests of the kingdom and its people. There was also a governing council who helped with kingdom affairs and kept everything running smoothly. The people were safe and happy. Many of them had only known this one king.

These were good times.

But everything changed one day, after the king had a dream. This dream convinced him it was time for him to leave. It was time for someone else to lead the kingdom. He immediately summoned the council and shared this news.

All the councilors were in shock but soon realized that they could not convince the king to stay. The council set out to replace the king and told everyone in the kingdom about the search.

As word spread throughout the kingdom, the citizens experienced different emotions about this situation: shock, anger, denial, fear, and even depression. But there was no opportunity to discuss these feelings. The citizens were never given a chance to celebrate all they had achieved under the king. They had to hold in their concerns for the kingdom, their feelings about the old king, and their hopes for the future. The council was too busy replacing the king to worry about such things. In fact, all normal kingdom business was interrupted, as all efforts were devoted to finding a new king.

In time, many neighboring princes were invited to visit the kingdom. Many citizens picked their favorite among the princes and argued about who they thought should become king. There wasn't any consensus, and the process caused greater confusion, disunity, and anxiety.

To make matters worse, while these prince visits were going on, some of the shopkeepers held a secret meeting to discuss the situation. They concluded that kings were too old-fashioned and decided the constitution should be changed to let the council run the kingdom. Besides, this would reduce taxes and make all the business owners happy!

Amidst all this emotion, excitement, and confusion, a wise stranger came to visit the kingdom. Having seen this sort of turmoil in other kingdoms, he went to the palace steps, gathered everyone around, and boldly announced:

Everyone! You have missed the point. Replacing the king is the wrong place to begin. You should start with yourselves. You have an opportunity to rediscover who you are, what kind of kingdom you are, and what kind of kingdom you want to be. Only when you know what kind of kingdom you want to be can you ever hope to find the right king to lead you there.

The citizens and the council heeded this advice and asked the wise stranger for his help. As the stranger talked to the people, he found out about all the strengths and challenges within the kingdom. The stranger was able to challenge the way some things had been done up till then. He helped some people overcome their fear of change and kept everyone focused on what the future of the kingdom should be.

After months of working with the stranger, the citizens were able to get over their disappointment over the old king leaving and their fear about the future. In fact, they were all excited about the future and had developed a good understanding of what kind of kingdom they wanted to be. Eventually, they found a new king who was well suited to lead them into the future, not just a replacement for their old king.

Before the stranger left, he joined in the old king's farewell celebration, including the dedication of a giant statue in front of the palace, which would forever recall the king's glorious reign.

At the dedication, the king revealed the details of his dream: it was a vision of two possible futures facing the kingdom he so loved. The first possible future was a continuation of the current reality — more of the same — where the kingdom's potential was limited by his presence and everyone had grown tired and complacent. In the second possible future, relationships were revitalized, and a renewed vision for the kingdom was established. In this second future, everyone was spurred on to greater achievements under a new king.

It was the old king who had secretly sent for the wise stranger to come, once he had seen the mayhem created by his announcement that he was leaving.

After that, the citizens of the kingdom crowned their new king. Everyone knew he would be the perfect fit for everything the kingdom aspired to be.

And the people rejoiced and lived happily ever after... ☺

The moral of the story: During times of leadership transition, seize the opportunity to reshape your organization. These rare seasons allow for celebration of past achievements and closure from past disappointments. They are a critical time in which visions and priorities can be renewed. They set the stage for a healthy transition and the careful selection of the next leader.[1]

Section 1: The Transitional Ministry

"It's not so much that we're afraid of change or so in love with the old ways, but it's that place in between that we fear...it's like being between trapezes. It's Linus when his blanket is in the dryer. There's nothing to hold on to."

— Marilyn Ferguson

Times of pastoral transition are windows of opportunity. For a congregation that seizes the opportunity, they can be a transformational turning point toward greater health and mission effectiveness. Welcoming a new senior pastor to a healthy, functioning, spiritually renewed congregation is a goal worth pursuing!

The goal of transitional ministry during the time between pastors is to prepare a congregation for fruitful ministry under the leadership of the next pastor. In this section, we lay out in broad strokes a road map for navigating the time between pastors.

Chapter 1

The Better Way

There are two basic approaches to navigating a pastoral transition in a congregation. The first approach is the *traditional* or *typical interim* model. The second approach is the *intentional transitional* or *intentional interim* model. This book builds a case for the second approach but will discuss the first approach to illustrate how the two are different. In some situations, a typical interim approach may be appropriate, but in the modern world this seems to be true less and less of the time.

A key principle when working with congregations between pastors is to match the solution to the problem. There was a day when the solution found in the traditional or typical interim model worked effectively. That day, for the most part, seems to have passed. Significant numbers of churches are now plateaued or declining in health and require an intentional approach. If nothing else changes, it is likely that these churches will continue to plateau or decline after a new pastor is hired. Therefore, it is crucial for these churches to seize the opportunity that a pastoral transition offers.

The Traditional or Typical Interim Model

The traditional or typical interim model conveys a "hold the fort" mentality. It normally provides basic pastoral care, rites of passage, pulpit supply, the conducting of worship services, and short-term administration. Under this model, the interim leader is often an experienced pastor, but that leader tends to focus only on maintaining regular ministry activities while a search process gets under way.

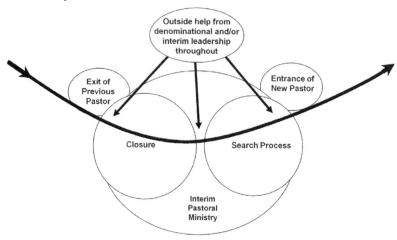

Figure 1: Traditional Interim Model

There are four phases of a traditional or typical interim ministry approach.

1. **The Exit** — The pastor exits for positive or negative reasons.

The exit is announced by the pastor, by a regional overseer, or by one of the congregational leaders. If the situation is awkward and negative, anxiety is a major emotion felt by the congregation.

The words heard by the congregation when the exit happens will probably include, "We will find a pastor as soon as possible." There is sometimes outside help to assist with the exit and aftermath—but not always.

2. **Closure** — The congregation comes to terms with the change, does some grieving, and gains a degree of hope for the future.

Closure in the traditional interim model varies depending on the skill set and experience of the leadership. There will be some opportunity for people to talk about their loss, but the extent to which this happens will depend entirely on the awareness and leadership abilities of those who are guiding the transition.

3. **Search Process** — The congregation begins the search for the next pastor.

In the traditional interim model, a search team is put in place near the beginning of the transitional period. This team will go to work by doing some evaluation and, as quickly as possible, preparing a church profile and pastor's job description to be used in a search.

The search team will put a positive face on the congregation even if the search team members know there are issues that need to be addressed. The church profile may not reflect the true picture of the congregation and its health. It may be written for the purpose of attracting a suitable candidate to the congregation who, the search team hopes, will be able to deal with the real issues.

The search process also includes the negotiation phase, in which the congregation interviews and assesses potential candidates. This will lead to a decision, and hopefully a suitable candidate will be found to join the congregation and lead it forward.

4. **Installation and Start-up** — The new pastor is welcomed into the congregation and begins ministry.

As the new pastor begins, hope is in the air, and the honeymoon starts. Pastor and people expect growth and new momentum to now happen.

If unresolved issues are under the surface, the new pastor will eventually bump into them and need to face them head on. If they cannot be worked through, the result may be another hasty exit and a pastor who unintentionally ends up being an interim pastor.

The Intentional Transitional Ministry Model

The *intentional transitional* or *intentional interim* model focuses on seeing the time between pastors as a season of renewal and opportunity, a time to facilitate meaningful and sustainable change.

In this model, the transitional leader is trained as a transitional specialist who prepares the congregation to conduct the search for a new pastor from a posture of health, prayer, and readiness. The focus of this model is on congregational health and vitality. It puts a high priority on getting the congregation ready for the entrance of the next pastor, not on filling the vacancy of the exiting pastor as quickly as possible.

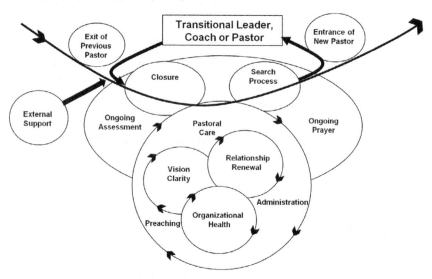

Figure 2: Intentional Transitional Model

In this model, eight goals provide a road map to guide the transitional process. These goals include facilitating closure, preaching, pastoral care, administration, relationship renewal, vision clarity, organizational health, and the search process. Each goal is explained in detail in Section 2 of this book.

Several principles and assumptions provide foundational support for an intentional transitional process.

1. There is a definite beginning and ending to the transitional ministry.

2. Clear transitional goals help create urgency and give clarity to the process.

3. Authority is given to the transitional leader to lead, facilitate, and coach the congregation in achieving the goals.

4. Responsibility is entrusted to the transitional leader to fulfill his or her duties with godly integrity.

5. Expectations about the transitional ministry are clearly stated and understood by the congregation, the congregational leaders, and the transitional leader.

6. Mutual accountability is emphasized and encouraged throughout the process.

7. Denominational co-operation and participation is encouraged and promoted to ensure a strong partnership going forward.

8. The search process is part of the transitional process, not central to it.

9. Planning is adapted to fit the congregational culture and context.

10. Ongoing training and equipping of transitional leaders ensures quality support and effective leadership for congregations.

The ultimate objective in the intentional transitional model is to hand off a healthier, spiritually renewed congregation to the incoming pastor. This enables the congregation to begin a new chapter of ministry unencumbered by issues from the past since these have been put to rest during the transitional process.

Why the Intentional Transitional Approach?

It's not enough to know *what* is involved in an intentional interim ministry. It is also important to know *why* it is worth the time and trouble to facilitate an intentional pastoral transition.

There are five potential benefits when a congregation embraces and steps into an intentional transitional process:

1. The intentional transitional model creates an atmosphere where renewal and healthy change are expected and potentially realized.

When a congregational culture is "unfrozen"[2] due to the exit of the previous pastor, an opportunity for change appears. New ways of thinking and behaving can emerge during the transition. On the heels of the changes that are made during the transition, there is an opportunity to "re-freeze" the new ways of thinking and behaving. This re-freezing can result in renewed enthusiasm and an excellent climate for a new pastor to step into.

2. The intentional transitional model provides an opportunity to bring in specialized leadership to work on specific tasks.

Transitional leadership is a specialized field. Not just any pastor can do this work well. The time between pastors provides both the salary room to hire an outside specialist and the opportunity for the congregation, without a senior pastor present, to look in the mirror, see what God sees, and adjust accordingly.

3. The intentional transitional model puts the focus on overall congregational health, preventing a premature pastoral search.

Jumping into a pastoral search too quickly can overshadow the need for an examination and treatment of health-impeding symptoms. Congregations that rush into a search often do so as a *reaction* to the vacuum created by a pastoral exit, not as a healthy *response* to the need to take the next step in the process.

Intentional transitional ministry slows the search process down and allows it to happen naturally. The better a congregation knows itself, how God is leading, and what kind of leader is needed going forward, the better the outcome will be.

4. **The intentional transitional model allows a congregation to embrace a transitional vision with clear goals and directed action.**

When a congregation has a clear transitional vision, the likelihood of the transition being productive will increase. Seneca said, "When a man does not know what harbor he is heading for, no wind is the right one."

A transitional vision is not a long-term, all-encompassing vision. It is rather a short-term picture of what the congregation needs to look like in order to move forward in health and strength with the next senior pastor.

5. **The intentional transitional model gives a congregation the opportunity to clean house and re-establish what's really important.**

From time to time, congregations need to clean out the cobwebs (outdated programs, unresolved conflicts) that have accumulated over time. The time between pastors provides an opportunity to discuss and deal decisively with sacred cows and elephants (those issues and problems the people all know are there but are either unwilling or unable to tackle).

One analogy is to call the transitional leader a garbage collector. Transitional leaders clean out the garbage collected in the house, take the bag of trash to the curb, and then leave. In this scenario, the incoming pastor won't have to deal with the clutter and debris that has already been taken out. The incoming pastor will have the freedom and the opportunity to start fresh in a clean house.

Reflective Questions

❖ What are the main differences between a traditional or typical approach to interim ministry and an intentional transitional interim ministry?

❖ What are the barriers you have noticed when convincing congregations to consider an intentional transitional approach to pastoral transition?

❖ Which of the benefits to the intentional transitional model resonates most for you?

Chapter 2

The View from 30,000 Feet

S eeing the bigger picture helps to fit the details into their proper perspective. This chapter looks at transitional ministry from the 30,000-foot level in order to paint with broad strokes the various components of transitional ministry. It first gives an overview of eight transitional goals, then discusses the type of leadership required to see those goals realized. Each area is developed more fully in later chapters.

The Transitional Goals

1. Facilitating Closure

Closure involves dealing with the past so that it does not hinder what God is wanting to do in the future. Closure begins the moment the previous pastor announces his or her exit and continues throughout the transition in diminishing degrees.

A transitional leader comes into the life of a congregation as a counselor and skilled listener, able to help individuals achieve closure. Issues faced during closure include celebrating the past, forgiving past hurts, holding on to the good, and letting go of past issues which keep people stuck.

2. Facilitating Preaching

Congregations in transition need to hear from God throughout their transition. Rather than old sermons unedited for this new season of ministry, people need to hear freshly minted messages from God that ring true and land squarely in hearts and lives.

Some transitional leaders are gifted communicators who fill the preaching role with excellence. Others are not; they should partner with others inside and outside the congregation to ensure that the people hear relevant and appropriate messages based on where they are in their transition.

3. Facilitating Pastoral Care

Another key element during a transition is loving pastoral care provided for both the leadership and the congregation. The amount and focus of the pastoral care will be determined by the type of transition the congregation is experiencing. The higher the stress, the greater the care needs will be.

The transitional leader needs to provide a certain amount of pastoral care but shouldn't be expected to *do* all the caring. He or she will work with others to ensure that the care needs of the congregation are met.

4. Facilitating Administration

During a pastoral transition, regular ministry needs to be organized in such a way as to ensure continuity and consistency. Administration is all about providing the organization necessary to support day-to-day ministry.

As in the other goal areas, if the transitional leader is not gifted in this area or assigned the role of administrator, it is essential to identify and put in place gifted partners to fill the need.

5. Facilitating Relationship Renewal

If meaningful and enduring change is to occur in the congregation during the time between pastors, it will often start in the area of relationship renewal. Relationship renewal refers to the relationship church members have with the Father, Son, and Holy

Spirit, with one another in the body of Christ, and with those outside the body of Christ.

The *agape* principle recognizes God's purpose for his people to be having a harmonious relationship with God, unity with one another in the body, and a genuine witness to those outside the body of Christ. Because unity and harmonious relations are God's purpose, every effort needs to be made to heal broken relationships and develop the same relational quality the members of the Trinity enjoy.

6. Facilitating Vision Clarity

Healthy congregations have a unique, God-sized vision for themselves. Not all visions need to be renewed, but, at the very least, all visions need periodic reviewing to ensure they are in step with the current ministry focus God has for the congregation.

If a vision is outdated and no longer relevant, the time between pastors can be a golden opportunity to take a fresh look at God's vision. Many congregations find it appropriate to start the vision-clarifying process during the transition but to complete the process after a new pastor is hired. This increases the level of ownership and motivation the future pastor will have toward implementing the vision.

7. Facilitating Organizational Health

This goal can have a wide range of applications depending on the context. At the heart of facilitating organizational health is an examination, evaluation, and adjustment of the systems, infrastructure, and policies of the congregation. This work requires matching the organization of the congregation to the purpose, values, and vision of the congregation.

Organizational health is about connectedness, not in terms of fellowship but in terms of the need to make sure the organization functions in a peaceful and orderly fashion. In the words of Paul, "God is not a God of disorder but of peace." (1 Corinthians 14:33 NIV)

8. Facilitating the Search Process

A healthy search takes place after a congregation achieves sufficient health, unity, and clarity to realize its true identity and the kind of pastor who should be invited into the community. At the beginning of a pastoral transition, it is critical to deal adequately with the anxiety often associated with the absence of a pastor. A skilled transitional leader can provide non-anxious leadership so the right process can precede the launch of a search.

Once a congregation is ready for the search, there are four phases to the process: preparation, documentation, exploration, and engagement. During these phases, it is paramount for the leadership to be spiritually sensitive to where God is at work in the congregation and in the heart and life of the one who will become the next pastor.

The Transitional Leader

Specialized leadership is needed to guide the congregation through the journey of pastoral transition. There are several qualities that a transitional leader must have in order to be able to help a congregation during this time. These qualities are summarized as the five Cs of character, competency, chemistry, capacity, and calling.

Character

Character is at the heart of the transitional leader. Character is who a person is in the closet and on the stage. Godly character is described in 1 Corinthians 13, where Paul defines *agape* love. Using 1 Corinthians 13 to describe the transitional leader, we could put it this way: The transitional leader displays patience, kindness, humility, respectfulness, selflessness, forgiveness, honesty, and commitment. These qualities grow and develop as the leader increases in self-awareness and practices the disciplines necessary to cultivate them.

Competency

Transitional leaders require a certain skill set and certain abilities and behaviors to do their job well. The primary core competencies required for effective transitional leadership include leading, coaching, shepherding, facilitating, managing conflict, managing change, and communicating.

Chemistry

Chemistry is about how well the transitional leader fits the context and culture he or she is going into. It involves values, mindset, and worldview. It is evident when both parties say, "I can't explain it, but we just click." Chemistry is somewhat intangible in nature and is assessed more by the *feel* of the connection between the transitional leader and the congregation. Good chemistry produces the ability to quickly gel as a team, reduces tension and potential conflict, and helps create an enjoyable work environment.

Capacity

Capacity includes having the experience to handle a transitional assignment and the ability to handle the size and complexity of the particular congregation the leader is going into. Capacity includes the ability to work within the distinctives of the particular denomination the congregation belongs to. It also involves being available to travel if the opportunity is away from home, having enough time to give the assignment the attention it needs, and having spousal support for the assignment.

Calling

In order for a pastor to be effective in transitional ministry, God's call to this work is essential. Transitional ministry is not just a "job" enabling the leader to earn a paycheck but is an expression of the grace of God working through the leader's life. Transitional leadership is a spiritual ministry, and being "called" is necessary to sustain the leader during tough meetings and hard conversations. The results of a "call" will be meaningful ministry and lasting fruit.

Reflective Questions

- ❖ What is the significance of using the word *facilitating* when describing the eight goals of a transition?

- ❖ What metaphor would you use to describe the transitional process?

- ❖ What would you consider the main leadership strengths required for effective transitional ministry?

Chapter 3

Ten Spiritual Building Blocks

E ffective transitional ministry is not a human undertaking. It is God-ordained, requiring both competent leadership and spiritual power. When both elements are present, the congregation increases its capacity to move from where it is to where God wants it to be. Without God's help and power, transitional ministry may produce short-term change but result in long-term disappointment and pain. The church is a living and breathing organism, not just an organization. It needs God's daily sustenance to maintain vitality and health.

As a congregation navigates the turbulent waters during the time between pastors, it's important for the congregation to have a foundation to stand on. This chapter lays down the spiritual foundation on which everything is built. If these principles are built into every step and phase of the transition, the chances of success rise exponentially.

Building Block 1: Faith

Transitional ministry is a faith journey. By faith, Christians trust in God's ability to lead and guide during times of uncertainty, chaos, and change. By faith, congregations and their transitional leaders trust God to help them map out a plan and give them the wisdom and courage to carry out the plan:

The fundamental fact of existence is that this trust in God, this faith, is the firm foundation under everything that makes life worth living. It's our handle on what we can't see. The act of faith is what distinguished our ancestors, set them above the crowd. (Hebrews 11:1-2 TM)

Henry Ward Beecher said, "Every tomorrow has two handles. We can take hold of it with the handle of anxiety or the handle of faith."

Building Block 2: Hope

The dictionary has two meanings for the word "hope": a) desire or expectation for something in the future to occur and b) grounds for believing something in the future will occur. We run into trouble when we have one without the other—when we have "desire" without any "grounds," when hope is not based on reality but only on our desires.

Oh! May the God of green hope fill you up with joy, fill you up with peace, so that your believing lives, filled with the life-giving energy of the Holy Spirit, will brim over with hope! (Romans 15:13 TM)

When we use hope in our everyday language, it is often soft. For example, we say, "I hope it rains" or "I hope they call with a job offer." Soft hope is an expectation with no grounds for believing. It is only a wish, not true hope.

The biblical word for hope is solid and strong. In the Bible, hope means "to look forward with confidence." Biblical hope is a guarantee that something will happen in the future. It is not an empty wish but an expectation, with reason to believe it will happen. This promise of a guaranteed future can be seen in Isaiah 40:30-31 (NIV):

"Even youths grow tired and weary, and young men stumble and fall; but those who hope in the LORD will renew their strength. They will soar on wings like eagles;

they will run and not grow weary, they will walk and not be faint."

Building Block 3: Love

"Love" means many different things. It can be soft and associated with emotions and feelings, or it can be strong and refer to a commitment to action. The Bible uses a strong Greek word for love: *agape*. *Agape* has its source in God. It is unconditional in nature. Transitional ministry needs leaders and participants who practice *agape*.

Love is the greatest commandment in Scripture, so it is only fitting to lay it down as one of the foundational blocks of transitional ministry:

One of them, an expert in the law, tested him with this question: "Teacher, which is the greatest commandment in the Law?" Jesus replied: "'Love the Lord your God with all your heart and with all your soul and with all your mind.' This is the first and greatest commandment. And the second is like it: 'Love your neighbor as yourself.' All the Law and the Prophets hang on these two commandments." (Matthew 22:35-40 NIV)

Love is the binding agent or glue holding everything and everyone together:

"Therefore, as God's chosen people, holy and dearly loved, clothe yourselves with compassion, kindness, humility, gentleness and patience. Bear with each other and forgive whatever grievances you may have against one another. Forgive as the Lord forgave you. And over all these virtues put on love, which binds them all together in perfect unity." (Colossians 3:12-14 NIV)

Building Block 4: Power

One New Year's Day, in the Tournament of Roses parade, an elaborate float suddenly sputtered and quit. The whole parade was held up until someone could get a can of gas to this float, owned and operated by the Standard Oil Company. In spite of this company's vast oil resources, the company had failed to provide enough gas to power its float.

Congregations in need of change and transformation sit on vast reserves of spiritual power. The key is to tap into the power available in the Holy Spirit:

> But you will receive power when the Holy Spirit comes on you; and you will be my witnesses in Jerusalem, and in all Judea and Samaria, and to the ends of the earth. (Acts 1:8 NIV)

The portal into God's reservoir of spiritual power is learning to daily remain in Christ and the power of his Holy Spirit:

> Remain in me, and I will remain in you. No branch can bear fruit by itself; it must remain in the vine. Neither can you bear fruit unless you remain in me. I am the vine; you are the branches. If a man remains in me and I in him, he will bear much fruit; apart from me you can do nothing. (John 15:4-5 NIV)

Building Block 5: Truth

The difference between Truth (with a capital "T") and truth (with a small "t") is the difference between God's Word and our opinion. Transitional ministry is rooted in capital "T" Truth— God's Word.

We will not find answers to every single question about transitional ministry in the pages of Scripture. We will find unchanging principles and directions for the pathway forward:

> There's nothing like the written Word of God for showing you the way to salvation through faith in Christ Jesus.

Every part of Scripture is God-breathed and useful one way or another—showing us truth, exposing our rebellion, correcting our mistakes, training us to live God's way. Through the Word we are put together and shaped up for the tasks God has for us. (2 Timothy 3:15-17 TM)

Building Block 6: Wisdom

Wisdom comes from a wide variety of places. It comes when we combine knowledge with evaluated experience. Wisdom is a gift from God, is present in the person of Jesus Christ, and is in us through the presence of the Holy Spirit:

For the LORD grants wisdom! From his mouth come knowledge and understanding. He grants a treasure of common sense to the honest. He is a shield to those who walk with integrity. He guards the paths of the just and protects those who are faithful to him. Then you will understand what is right, just, and fair, and you will find the right way to go. For wisdom will enter your heart, and knowledge will fill you with joy. Wise choices will watch over you. Understanding will keep you safe. (Proverbs 2:6-11 NLT)

Theologian J.I. Packer said, "Wisdom is the power to see and the inclination to choose the best and highest goal, together with the surest means of attaining it."

Building Block 7: Purpose

God invites his followers to join him on his mission—the task of making disciples of all nations (more disciples and better disciples). When a congregation loses sight of its mission and purpose, it's time for change.

During pastoral transitions, the lack of alignment with God's purpose often surfaces. When it does, an opportunity emerges for the leadership and the congregation to find out what God is doing and join him in living out his purpose in fresh and new ways.

> When they saw him, they worshiped him; but some doubted. Then Jesus came to them and said, "All authority in heaven and on earth has been given to me. Therefore go and make disciples of all nations, baptizing them in the name of the Father and of the Son and of the Holy Spirit, and teaching them to obey everything I have commanded you. And surely I am with you always, to the very end of the age." (Matthew 28:17-20 NIV)

Building Block 8: Leadership

Whenever God needs to bring about change, he raises up godly leaders to lead the charge. The Bible is full of examples of leaders God used to take his people from where they were to where he wanted them to be. Moses, Aaron, David, Esther, Isaiah, Peter, John, and countless others are in the list. These leaders weren't perfect, but they were willing to serve and were available for the work God wanted them to do:

> Here are the stages in the journey of the Israelites when they came out of Egypt by divisions under the leadership of Moses and Aaron. (Numbers 33:1 NIV)
> Samuel took the horn of oil and anointed him in the presence of his brothers, and from that day on the Spirit of the LORD came upon David in power. (1 Samuel 16:13 NIV)
> I [Nehemiah] set out during the night with a few men. I had not told anyone what my God had put in my heart to do for Jerusalem. (Nehemiah 2:12 NIV)
> [Mordecai:] "Do not think that because you are in the king's house you alone of all the Jews will escape. For if you remain silent at this time, relief and deliverance for the Jews will arise from another place, but you and your father's family will perish. And who knows but that you

have come to your royal position for such a time as this?" [Esther:] "Do not eat or drink for three days, night or day. I and my attendants will fast as you do. When this is done, I will go to the king, even though it is against the law. And if I perish, I perish." (Esther 4:12-16 NIV)

When they saw the courage of Peter and John and realized that they were unschooled, ordinary men, they were astonished and they took note that these men had been with Jesus. (Acts 4:13 NIV)

Spiritual leadership is challenging, but when God is in it, success is possible. Henry and Richard Blackaby describe the leader's task this way: "The spiritual leader's task is to move people from where they are to where God wants them to be."

J. Oswald Sanders, speaking about spiritual leadership, says, "There is no such thing as a self-made spiritual leader. He is able to influence others spiritually only because the Spirit is able to work in and through him to a greater degree than in those whom he leads."[3]

Building Block 9: Trust

Trust has to do with honesty and integrity. Without trust, transitional ministry will not succeed. Trust in this sense refers to trust in God as well as the trust people have in each other. Trusting one another is characterized by openness and honesty wrapped in love. It's the opposite of someone who perpetually lies:

Don't lie to each other, for you have stripped off your old sinful nature and all its wicked deeds. Put on your new nature, and be renewed as you learn to know your Creator and become like him. (Colossians 3:9-10 NLT)

Organizational guru Peter Drucker gives this wisdom: "Trust is the conviction that the leader means what he or she says. It is a belief in two old-fashioned qualities called consistency and integrity. Trust opens the door to change." George MacDonald said it another way: "Few delights can equal the presence of one whom we trust utterly."

Building Block 10: Change

God is in the business of transforming the lives of people who will transform organizations. When Jesus appeared on the scene, he came to an outdated and brittle structure unable to hold the new wine of his Spirit and kingdom:

> And no one puts new wine into old wineskins. For the old skins would burst from the pressure, spilling the wine and ruining the skins. New wine is stored in new wineskins so that both are preserved. (Matthew 9:16-17 NLT)

When the structures we have built grow old and brittle, God desires to bring renewal and transformation to the way we organize what he is doing. The time between pastors is an opportunity to consider what the new wineskins should look like so that they will be ready when God again pours out his Spirit on his church.

A congregation that is stagnant, unproductive, and unfruitful needs the wind of God's Spirit to blow afresh. But before that will happen, the congregation will have to admit that the air is stale and needs to be replaced.

Reflective Questions

❖ What happens when transitional ministry is carried out without a solid spiritual foundation?

❖ What are some ways to build into a congregation the spiritual building blocks described in this chapter?

❖ What passages of Scripture would you use to help lay a spiritual foundation for pastoral transition?

Section 2: The Transitional Goals

"Set positive goals and reasonable expectations."

— Steve Strasser

G oals during a pastoral transition are critical because they give focus to the work needing to be done. There are eight areas to be addressed during a pastoral transition: closure, preaching, pastoral care, administration, relationship renewal, vision clarity, organizational health, and the search process.

The role of the transitional leader is to facilitate achieving specific goals in each of these areas. The order of the goals is intentional and follows the typical progression in a healthy transitional journey. A congregation may, however, need to revisit a goal area thought to be completed because new information has come to light. While this may appear to be a setback, it should be embraced as a necessary part of the process.

Chapter 4

Facilitating Closure

C losure means "to close or shut, to bring something to an end or conclusion." It involves accepting the past and facing the present reality, closing the door on the past and opening the door to the future. Closure during pastoral transitions involves finding a pathway to recover from past problems and hurts. It involves dealing with legitimate issues from the past on the basis of justice, mercy, and forgiveness. It requires letting go of the past in order to take hold of the future.

Biblical Examples of Closure

Scripture is full of examples encouraging closure in the lives of God's people. Paul speaks about letting go in order to hang on:

> Brothers, I do not consider myself yet to have taken hold of it. But one thing I do: Forgetting what is behind and straining toward what is ahead, I press on toward the goal to win the prize for which God has called me heavenward in Christ Jesus. (Philippians 3:13-14 NIV)

Israel was told to remember the lessons of the past in order to know how to live in the present and future:

> Remember how the LORD your God led you all the way in the desert these forty years, to humble you and to test you in order to know what was in your heart, whether or not you would keep his commands...Know then in your heart that as a man disciplines his son, so the LORD your God disciplines you. (Deuteronomy 8:2-5 NIV)

The future for God's people was rooted in their past but shaped by the new work God was going to do. To get to their future, they had to leave their past behind and follow the Lord in faith.

> For the LORD your God is bringing you into a good land—a land with streams and pools of water, with springs flowing in the valleys and hills; a land with wheat and barley, vines and fig trees, pomegranates, olive oil and honey; a land where bread will not be scarce and you will lack nothing; a land where the rocks are iron and you can dig copper out of the hills. (Deuteronomy 8:7-9 NIV)

There are three examples in Scripture of how closure was facilitated during leadership transitions.

- **Moses to Joshua:**

> After the death of Moses the servant of the LORD, the LORD said to Joshua son of Nun, Moses' aide: "Moses my servant is dead. Now then, you and all these people, get ready to cross the Jordan River into the land I am about to give to them—to the Israelites…Be strong and courageous. Do not be terrified; do not be discouraged, for the LORD your God will be with you wherever you go." (Joshua 1:1-9 NIV)

- **David to Solomon:**

> Then David said to the whole assembly, "Praise the LORD your God."…Then they acknowledged Solomon son of David as king a second time…So Solomon sat on the throne of the LORD as king in place of his father David. He prospered and all Israel obeyed him. All the officers and mighty men, as well as all of King David's sons, pledged their submission to King Solomon. (1 Chronicles 29:20-25 NIV)

- **The ministry of Jesus to the work of the apostles:**

> "But you will receive power when the Holy Spirit comes on you; and you will be my witnesses in Jerusalem, and in

all Judea and Samaria, and to the ends of the earth." After he said this, he was taken up before their very eyes, and a cloud hid him from their sight. (Acts 1:8, 9 NIV)

Thoughtful Anticipation...Letting Go to Take Hold!

The group stood before the history wall with thoughtful anticipation. They had just spent twenty minutes in reflection, as each member recalled and wrote down three personal highlights and three low points of their life experience in this congregation. They were now looking at ten years of personal emotional history of their community of faith. There were clusters of highlights around the hiring of a youth pastor and the summer camps they had held for street kids.

On the other side, there were clusters of low points around the exit of the previous pastor (four years earlier) and the building project that had gone wrong. The members were asked to make some observations (not draw conclusions) about their collective history. At one point, a long-time member pointed out how the majority of the low points seemed to cluster around some ongoing hurt over the exit of the previous pastor. There was general consensus that the congregation was still stuck in this past event.

A newer member asked if this might be the reason why they had not been successful in getting a new pastor in the past four years. After considerable conversation around these feelings of being stuck, the facilitator asked, "What would it take to move this congregation forward?"

At this point, two members asked for forgiveness for holding a grudge against the elders who had removed the previous pastor. The elders responded by granting forgiveness and then asked for forgiveness for their part in a poorly managed process during the exit of the previous pastor. Tears flowed; hugs followed.

There was a sweet sense of Holy Spirit closure to the past and a renewed sense of hope for the future God was going to unveil for this congregation.

— Alan Simpson

Why Closure Is Necessary and Worthwhile

There are several reasons why closure is both necessary and worthwhile. At the core, helping a congregation deal with its past is critical so the past does not negatively impact the future.

> After a fruitful ministry, members may grieve the loss of the previous pastor or even be at war with each other over his departure. Regardless of the circumstances, lack of closure prohibits a congregation from moving on.

Closure is as necessary to navigating a pastoral transition as a set of locks is for a ship navigating an uneven waterway. In order for the ship to reach its destination, it must pass through one lock at a time. It must move through one door, wait for it to close, allow the water to lift the ship up or down to the new level, then wait for the door to open into the next lock before continuing. The ship cannot rush the journey or jump the gates. It must allow one door to shut before the next door can open. The congregation in transition is moving from one level to another. It cannot get to the next level by jumping the gates or rushing the process. It must move in stages to the next level before it can begin its journey towards new opportunities.

An effective tool often used to take this journey is the history wall. It allows for a holy conversation about the past, covering both the high points and the painful memories.

Taking time to stop and think about the journey so far gives the congregation an opportunity to celebrate the best of the past. Looking at its history and reflecting on it can prevent a congregation from repeating the mistakes of the past. It can also remind the congregation of values and principles that it might want to revisit and relearn. God, in his wisdom, told the Israelites to remember what God had done as a way of reminding them of his ability to do the work again in their present and future.

If traumatic events have shaped a congregation's past and caused pain, forgetting about them is not the best remedy.

Psychiatrist Alan Manevitz of New York's Lenox Hill Hospital worked with patients following 9/11. He discovered it was much better in the long run to remember bad events than forget about them. Facilitating closure allows hurtful memories and unresolved issues within a congregation to be dealt with and deeply healed. Jumping the gates of closure will cause the congregation to miss out on the powerful healing God has in mind for his church.

The process of closure gives members of a congregation the time to reflect on the past, deal with losses and wounds, and express gratitude.

Three Types of Pastoral Exits and Their Effect on Closure

Not all pastoral exits are equal in intensity and impact. They come in all shapes and sizes but generally fall into three categories.

1. A Smooth Exit

A smooth exit occurs when the pastor leaves on good terms and the congregation sustains limited or no damage to relational health or ministry impact. The pastor may be retiring, taking on a different ministry assignment, or leaving for some other reason that is not negative in nature.

It's important to remember that even in a smooth exit, loss is still experienced, and the congregation requires time to grieve and recover from the loss. Pain, emptiness, and loneliness will be present to various degrees, depending on how close people were to the pastor and his family. The pastor who was there for the members in various crises, officiated at their children's weddings, and equipped them for ministry is now gone. A hole has been left behind.

The transitional leader needs to be able to identify when congregation members are still grieving. Do people still talk about the former pastor, remember things said and done, and tearfully remember the "good old days"? Are they consumed with a longing for the pastor's return? To the degree that the door to the past is open, it will impact the amount of work and length of time needed for healthy closure.

2. A Rough Exit

A rough exit is when the pastor leaves under stressful circumstances, resulting in damage or disruption to relationships and ministry. It is less intense and traumatic than a crisis exit but still results in negative emotions requiring special attention.

A rough exit may be caused by unresolved conflict, a forced exit of the pastor by the leaders of the congregation, a personal crisis in the pastor's life such as burnout, or the pastor announcing the exit with very little explanation as to why.

When the transitional leader arrives in this kind of situation, the leader must assess the degree to which the door to the past is still open and act accordingly. There will be tender hearts and disappointed people, but there will also be those who were out of harm's way and who are eager to move forward. The leader must convince the congregation of the value of traveling together through closure before starting to prepare for the future.

3. A Crisis Exit

A crisis exit is when the pastor leaves because of an indiscretion, betrayal, or misconduct. It's more traumatic than a rough exit and involves sin and deep disappointment on various levels.

A crisis exit might involve misappropriation of funds, sexual misconduct, or abuse of power and authority. There might be a legal challenge, an impending lawsuit, or the involvement of outside parties in the process. The transitional leader may need to call upon other specialists to help navigate such a crisis situation.

When a transitional leader comes to work with a congregation in crisis, great discernment and wisdom are necessary. There may be deep wounding, broken relationships, disillusioned people, and severely stressed people in the congregation and leadership. The door to the past is wide open. Bringing closure to such a situation will require justice, biblical peacemaking, and deep healing.

The Role of Grief during Closure

Healthy closure requires acknowledging and dealing with the grief experienced when the previous pastor left. The Kubler-Ross model is useful for understanding the process of grief. This model suggests that those who have experienced a loss or ending go

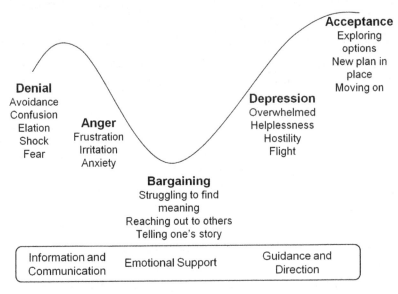

Acceptance
Exploring
options
New plan in
place
Moving on

Denial
Avoidance
Confusion
Elation
Shock
Fear

Anger
Frustration
Irritation
Anxiety

Depression
Overwhelmed
Helplessness
Hostility
Flight

Bargaining
Struggling to find
meaning
Reaching out to others
Telling one's story

Information and Communication	Emotional Support	Guidance and Direction

Figure 3: Kubler-Ross Grief Cycle

through five stages of the grief cycle—denial, anger, bargaining, depression, and acceptance—although not necessarily in that order. As people move through the stages, they require information, emotional support, and guidance.

The transitional leader can facilitate a process of understanding as the congregation and its leaders travel through the stages of grief, loss, and recovery. One way to facilitate this discovery process is to explain the grief cycle and then use carefully crafted questions to guide the participants in a conversation. Here are some questions that could be asked:

- Where do you see yourself in the grief cycle?
- Where do you think the congregation is in this grief cycle?
- How can we give permission to one another and be OK with where we are at in the grief cycle?
- If you feel you have moved through the grief cycle, what can you offer to those who are still in the middle of their grief?
- What do we need from others to help us move forward through the grieving process?

When grief is not managed well, various symptoms can be seen to be emerging within the congregation. They include:

- **Self-absorption** — a preoccupation with self to the exclusion of others
- **Overt anxiety** — uneasiness and apprehension regarding the future
- **Resentfulness** — bitterness, indignation, or anger towards others or towards God
- **Guilt** — self-reproach for failures or wrongdoing in the past
- **Stress** — physical, mental, or emotional
- **Blame** — holding others responsible for the past and finding fault with them for present pain
- **Unforgiveness** — not letting go of past offenses even when they have been acknowledged by the offending party

If these symptoms are present in the congregation, the whole body is affected to some degree. Paul said, "If one part hurts, every other part is involved in the hurt, and in the healing" (1 Corinthians 12:26 TM).

If the grieving process is not managed well, it will hinder the congregation from moving forward and may also cause members of the congregation to loop back to unhealthy norms when the next pastor is hired. This will increase the potential for sin and dysfunction; sin leads to death and more grief and loss.

The Stages of Closure

William Bridges, in his book *Managing Transitions,* highlights three main stages of a transition. The strength of this model is that it focuses on the internal process of transition and not the external event of change. It also recognizes that individuals (and groups within the congregation) will process transition at their own pace. The three stages people experience when they go through a transition are an ending stage, a neutral stage, and a new beginning stage. The role of the transitional leader is to help people navigate through these stages.

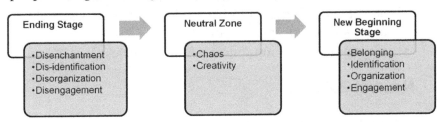

Figure 4: The Stages of Closure

Ending Stage

The ending stage unfolds in various ways. It begins with a conversation acknowledging that the old way of life has come to an end. Something is gone and cannot be recovered. To have an ending, the congregation must experience closure individually and corporately. It is often helpful to have rites of passage such as services specifically honoring the past and welcoming the future. Also useful are tangible activities such as a history wall. Tangible activities help a congregation see where "here" is so they can eventually start to move towards "there."

Here are ways the transitional leader can facilitate the ending stage:

- Determine who is letting go of what—be specific and allow others to define their unique perspectives.
- Help the congregation accept the loss and process the accompanying grief.
- Use preaching to give a biblical framework to the place of closure in the journey of the people of God.
- Initiate open dialogue about the emotions people may be feeling.
- Focus on problems to be solved rather than on people to be blamed.
- Provide opportunities for the congregation to process past issues and areas where they are stuck.
- Find ways to heal old wounds. Keep at it until people start to say they are tired of dealing with the past and are ready to start moving on.
- Communicate, communicate, communicate!

Neutral Zone

The neutral zone will often be filled with feelings of emptiness or confusion. There is a need to surrender to this feeling of emptiness or chaos. It's OK not to have answers. This is seen by some as the season when people are *unfrozen* from previous norms but not yet ready to *refreeze* into the new way of doing things. If future new beginnings are ever going to emerge, there must be a willingness to embrace the transformational power of being in neutral, of dwelling for a time in the space between where people were and where they hope to be.

Here are ways a transitional leader can facilitate the passage through the neutral zone:

- In a safe environment, talk about people's experiences, actions, and feelings in this neutral zone.
- Minimize other changes during this transitional stage.

- Be reassuring and patient while providing support and encouragement.
- Stay visible and present as the facilitator, counselor, and coach.
- Monitor signs of distress, and address what may be helping or hindering the shift through the neutral zone.
- Listen for the forward-moving language of dreaming or the imagining of new possibilities.

New Beginning

The initial indication of readiness for a new beginning is in how language starts to change. People stop talking about the past and begin dreaming about future possibilities. There is often a new energy for ministry and a new sense of direction. People start to feel they are entering a new chapter in their lives. A new hope is springing up, and creative energy is readily available to accept new challenges.

Here are ways a transitional leader can facilitate new beginnings:

- Help the leaders and the congregation communicate their new dreams and visions, develop new strategies, and define their roles as they engage in new or renewed ministries.
- Identify and celebrate small wins as individuals and the congregation progress.
- Identify resources that can enhance the desire to move forward into the future.
- Find ways to provide the knowledge, skill training, and reproducible models that can help launch new ideas effectively.
- Build self-esteem and confidence through personal and congregational encouragement.

Three Hurdles to Get Over When Facilitating Closure

1. Unresolved past issues affecting future actions

Unresolved issues in individuals and the congregation interfere with current and future ministry effectiveness. They prohibit enthusiasm for transitioning to a preferred future.

Overcoming this hurdle requires transparency in a safe environment. The transitional leader should create safe places where the leaders and the congregation can talk through their past issues without blaming or shaming.

2. Unresolved resentment siphoning off energy for life and ministry

Unrealized longings and resentments due to past issues siphon off energy and take away the ability to receive God's power to work. When Israel left Egypt, the rose-colored view the Israelites retained of their past was a hindrance to their march toward the Promised Land.

When Israel stood on the edge of the Jordan, the Israelites were finally ready to claim their inheritance from God. They were also ready as a new people for a new leader with a new vision.

3. A fixation on the past, hindering the ability to love in the present

Fixating on certain aspects of the past can get in the way of loving others in the present. A fixation on past words and actions that resulted in unresolved resentment and bitterness can play havoc with present relationships. These situations require *agape* love and grace to be resolved.

Those aspects deserving of honor and remembrance that were pivotal in shaping the congregation's identity deserve to keep a place in the congregation's ongoing story. The key is to close the door on unhealthy aspects while keeping the door open on life-giving memories and events.

42

Some Final Thoughts on Facilitating Closure

The transitional leader, as a facilitator of the closure process, must listen well, ask powerful questions, and be a non-anxious presence. The leader must also have access to the appropriate tools and know how to use them in a timely way. Closure can be messy due to the emotions that are often involved at this stage of transition.

Below is a list of ideas to keep in mind when facilitating closure. Not all of these ideas will be applicable to every situation, but they can be helpful in designing the path to closure.

- Assess the level of stress and emotional pain through formal and informal assessment tools.
- Work with the transition team and other leaders to make prayer an integral part of the closure process.
- Work together with the congregational leaders and the transition team to design a collaborative approach.
- Teach, preach, and encourage closure at every opportunity.
- Hold up as praiseworthy the faith and obedience of past members and leaders of the congregation.
- When there is a cloud of secrecy over why the previous pastor left, find a way to communicate adequate information to those confused without breaking confidentiality agreements.
- Identify problems or mistakes from the past, and extract any valuable lessons that can be learned from those mistakes.
- Press for the resolution of any unresolved issues from the past, and design a process to deal with them biblically and decisively.
- Provide clearly defined opportunities for the congregation to officially leave the past behind and move forward together.
- Build short-term closure goals with a plan for implementation.

Reflective Questions

❖ What biblical stories would you use to illustrate closure?

❖ What issues might be faced when facilitating closure?

❖ What approaches and strategies would you use to help a congregation and its leadership deal with closure?

A Story of Closure

John came to Valley Church with high expectations. He had moved his family halfway across the country to one of the most beautiful western communities he had ever seen. Both he and the congregation had high hopes for a fruitful ministry together.

Before long, many in the congregation realized this was not a good match. John's cultural background and experience were very different. He admitted he gave little effort to sermon preparation and confessed to scraping the bottom of his old sermon barrel for messages.

After struggling for a few years, John resigned and, in his anger, refused a farewell service. In an attempt to support John and his family in their transition, the leaders, along with some members, offered to help load the truck for the move back to their previous home. When they arrived at the parsonage to help load the truck, to their utter shock, they discovered that the house was empty and the truck and family were gone. They had loaded the truck by themselves during the night and had driven off without saying goodbye to anyone in the church.

When the district minister heard this tragic story during a consultation with the board, he knew that something had to be done. The congregation needed help to deal with the guilt experienced over the disastrous closure of John's ministry. He explained it was very important for them to close the last chapter with John and his family. If they didn't, bad feelings would carry over into the next chapter and create difficulties for the church and the next pastor.

Before a new chapter could be written successfully in the history of this congregation, the congregation would need to find a way to close the last chapter effectively.

Together, they worked out a plan to raise funds to pay for the former pastor's move. With no church to go to, John and his family had moved a great distance at their own expense. The district minister further advised the board not to quietly send a check to the former pastor, but to get the whole congregation involved in the decision and in raising the funds. This gave all members of the church a chance to work through their own pain in the process.

As Valley Church worked through this process and put a generous check in the mail, the congregation put closure to a painful experience. It helped the church close one chapter and begin opening a new chapter without carrying this unresolved issue forward. It also helped John and his family move on with their lives, which they thankfully did as well.

Bringing closure to a bad experience is absolutely essential before a church can move forward to an exciting new ministry. When old issues are not resolved, they will rise up and cause damage at unexpected times—in often totally unrelated ways. A current pastor's hands may be tied because of unresolved issues with the predecessor. If the former pastor was wasteful with money, the next pastor may be watched like a hawk and be unable to gain trust in the area of money. When calling a new pastor, churches often look for opposite traits instead of looking at the current needs of the church.

Every wise candidating pastor should explore how the previous pastor fared in the church. Then, with that background, the new pastor can build on his strengths, deal with overhanging shadows, and not suffer unnecessarily for the previous pastor's weaknesses and errors.

– Abe Funk

Chapter 5

Facilitating Preaching

C ommunication through preaching and teaching is a key element in a successful and harmonious transition. It is one powerful way to help the congregation see the opportunity embedded in the transitional process. Preaching provides a way to connect Scripture with God's desire to see his church renewed and empowered by his Spirit.

As the transitional leader facilitates the preaching ministry during a transition, it's important that the preaching offers fresh messages from God for the congregation. If the sermons preached come from the sermon archives and are delivered exactly as they were delivered the first time they were preached, the congregation will miss God's relevant word for *now*.

If the transitional leader is given the opportunity to preach, the leader should remember that the congregation needs hope, direction, and guidance as it navigates the transition. If a previously preached sermon is used, it should be adjusted and reworked so it breathes with fresh inspiration and application for the new situation.

This chapter provides a pathway for integrating the preaching task into the transitional vision and plan. For more on the planning process, see Chapter 22.

The Pathway for Facilitating Preaching

To make the task of facilitating preaching practical, there are three points to keep in mind: 1) peruse the preaching landscape; 2) plan the preaching themes; and 3) prompt the preaching participants.

1. Peruse the preaching landscape.

The place to begin is to get a clear picture of what is actually going on in the area of preaching. Every congregation has a certain culture and approach to the way God's Word is taught and preached in public services. The transitional leader should begin by trying to understand what preaching looks and feels like when he or she arrives. The leader should learn what is acceptable, common practice and what is frowned upon in the area of preaching.

Is a radically different approach to preaching a good way to shock a congregation and bring about change? It depends. Generally, it is better to learn more about what is before getting proactive in initiating change. Preaching communicates vision, teaches God's principles for living, and helps prepare the congregation for the journey of transition. Preaching is a place to sow seeds of hope and inspire people to change, but it requires other supportive initiatives for maximum impact. There will likely be a time to bring about change and introduce fresh thinking to the preaching task. However, that time is not likely to come when the transitional leader starts work but only after a time of discernment in partnership with the transition team and congregational leadership.

Here are a few questions to ask that will reveal the preaching landscape within the congregation.

- What kind of preaching is the congregation familiar with?
- What is the story people tell about the previous pastor's preaching?

- What is the best way to describe the culture of the services where preaching is carried out within the congregation?
- What is the level of biblical literacy in the congregation? What are the gaps?
- What are the core beliefs and doctrines of this congregation?

There are various methods and structures that can be used to gather information on the role and place of preaching in the congregation.

- During interviews, include specific questions about people's perspectives on the preaching.
- Ask staff members and the leadership community what they feel is a necessary direction for the preaching to go.
- As part of any survey of the congregation, make sure there are questions to assess perceptions and viewpoints on the preaching ministry.
- Listen to previous sermons.

2. Plan the preaching themes and schedule.

Facilitating the preaching includes developing a list of themes that is thought through and prayed over. It also includes developing a list of speakers who can work together to accomplish the goals of the transition. The transitional leader may be central to this ministry or simply a participant in it.

When designing the preaching topics and themes, what makes the preaching intentional and integrated with the transitional process is to match the preaching with the transitional goal the congregation is currently working through. For example, if the congregation is in the early stages of the transition, it is important to be sensitive to the need for closure and to realize that the people hearing the messages are in various stages of grief. This principle is equally true during other phases of the transitional process.

The following table provides sermon ideas for the various stages of the transitional process. This list of sermon ideas can serve as a way to kick-start sermon planning.

Goal Area and Timing	Theme or Title with Scripture
Closure (beginning and as needed)	"What Time Is It?" (Ecclesiastes 3:1-14) "God's New Way" (Isaiah 43:16-21) "The Best of Times – the Worst of Times" (Jeremiah 20) "Rebuilding a Broken Life" (Ruth) "Letting Go – Moving On" (Ruth) "Good Grief" (Lamentations) "True Blessings" (Matthew 5) "Emotions When We Say Goodbye" (Psalms)
Pastoral Care (beginning)	"Living with One Another" (Romans 15:1-7) "The Good Shepherd" (Psalm 23) "The Believers in Community" (Acts 2:42-47) "Clothes for Holy People" (Colossians 3:12-15)
Administration (any time)	"Gifts for the Body" (1 Corinthians 12; Ephesians 4) "Jethro Mentors Moses" (Exodus 18) "How Ministry Gets Done" (Acts 6) "Dividing up the Work" (Nehemiah)
Relationship Renewal (near beginning and throughout)	"Me or We?" (Philippians 2:1-5) "Fences Do Not Make Good Neighbors" (Ephesians 2) "The One Anothers" (various NT Scriptures) "The Peacemaker's Pledge" (Ephesians 4:1-2; Romans 12:18) "A Son Comes Home" (Luke 15) "Love Is a Verb" (1 Corinthians 13) "The Ministry of Reconciliation" (2 Corinthians 5)
Vision Clarity (half way through)	"God's Renovation" (Nehemiah) "The Church: Cruise Liner or Rescue Boat" (Matthew 28) "Where Are We Going?" "Look, Write, Run, Wait" (Habakkuk 2:1-3)
Organizational Health (half way through)	"He Appointed Elders" (Titus 1) "Functional Structures" (Acts 6) "New Wineskins Required" (Matthew 9:14-17) "The Speed of Trust" (1 Samuel 18) "Getting Your House in Order" (Ezra)
Search Process (mid-point or last half)	"A King Is Chosen" (1 Samuel 16) "The Qualities of an Elder" (Titus) "Praying for a Leader" (Acts 13) "Someone Takes His Place" (Acts 1:21-26)

Table 1: Preaching Themes During Transition

Who preaches does matter. The congregation needs to be protected from harmful, poorly timed, or poorly chosen sermons. The preaching quality will not always be consistent, depending on the pool of available speakers, but high quality biblical preaching should always be the goal.

When it comes to coordinating who speaks, there are a number of ways to arrange it. Here are a few options to consider:

- The transitional leader assumes the majority of the preaching and teaching responsibilities, with guest speakers or congregational members filling in from time to time.
- The transitional leader leads the transition and works in partnership with another leader, whose primary gift and responsibility is to provide preaching and teaching.
- The congregation fills the need for preaching through a team of rotating pastors and speakers.
- Some combination of the above.

3. Prompt the preaching process and participants.

The role of preaching during a transition is similar to the task of conducting an orchestra or singing group: "The primary duties of the conductor are to unify performers, set the tempo, execute clear preparations and beats, and to listen critically and shape the sound of the ensemble."[4]

Preaching during a transition should be used to unify the congregation and set the tempo of the transitional process. It should prepare people for change and help the congregation to be in sync with God's instructions, producing the notes God wants the congregation and leaders to play. The goal? To honor God and see his body healthy and whole.

Reflective Questions

❖ What are some ways you could assess the style and history of the preaching and teaching in a congregation?

❖ How is preaching different in the intentional interim model compared to the typical interim model?

❖ What is the main role of preaching during the time between pastors?

Chapter 6

Facilitating Pastoral Care

A nother essential element during the time between pastors is pastoral care. It's required for the leaders and the congregation. The transitional leader does not provide all the pastoral care but can be instrumental in helping to facilitate pastoral care.

A congregation in transition often needs special attention in the area of nurture and care due to the loss of the previous pastor. The kind of exit and the level of engagement people had with the previous pastor will often determine the type of care required.

Those giving pastoral care to the congregation, whether paid staff or members of the body caring for one another, serve as partners with the Holy Spirit. It's the Holy Spirit who empowers people to care deeply for each other.

The People who Provide Pastoral Care

Pastoral care is not just the work of professional clergy. It is ministry the whole body of Christ is involved with. There are certainly unique roles and activities for those in leadership when it comes to pastoral care, but not to the exclusion of the greater body.

As Christians, we all offer daily encouragement to one another: "But encourage one another daily, as long as it is called 'Today,' so that none of you may be hardened by sin's deceitfulness." (Hebrews 3:13 NIV) We also carry one another's burdens: "Carry each other's burdens, and in this way you will fulfill the law of Christ." (Galatians 6:2 NIV)

The role of leadership is to oversee the care of people — not as solo entrepreneur shepherds but as player-coaches who serve and coordinate. Peter said, "Keep watch over yourselves and all the flock of which the Holy Spirit has made you overseers. Be shepherds of the church of God, which he bought with his own blood." (Acts 20:28 NIV)

Peter offers further encouraging words to a people in the midst of adversity and transition. His words are full of practical suggestions on how to love and care for one another:

> Above all, love each other deeply, because love covers over a multitude of sins. Offer hospitality to one another without grumbling. Each of you should use whatever gift you have received to serve others, as faithful stewards of God's grace in its various forms. If anyone speaks, they should do so as one who speaks the very words of God. If anyone serves, they should do so with the strength God provides, so that in all things God may be praised through Jesus Christ. (1 Peter 4:8-11 NIV)

So who provides the care?

- staff members
- the transitional leader
- board members
- ministry leaders
- qualified and available members without an official position
- external resource people such as counselors, coaches, other pastors, denominational leaders, and members of other congregations
- the system of small groups and ministry teams caring for one another
- the body caring for one another organically and naturally

Why Care is Needed

Pastoral care during a pastoral transition depends on the situation. The needs should be determined by a careful assessment of the situation.

> "One of the highest of human duties is the duty of encouragement. There is a regulation of the Royal Navy which says: 'No officer shall speak discouragingly to another officer in the discharge of his duties.'" — William Barclay

In general terms, there are a few additional factors that may come into play when a congregation is going through a transition. It is possible that not all of these will be present, but it is wise to keep eyes and ears open to what the reality is.

- Individuals will be experiencing varying degrees of grief.

Many of the symptoms noticeable in people will be similar to the emotions of those who have lost a family member or friend. Other individuals will have milder symptoms of loneliness and insecurity.

- Leadership resources may be reduced.

Following a pastoral exit, leadership resources are reduced to some degree. Depending on the health and maturity of the leadership community, the actual resources in the area of pastoral care may or may not be significantly reduced.

If the actual care of people is reduced because they were close to the previous pastor or because his ministry was very hands-on in nature, the job of the transitional leader will be to fill the gap in practical ways. If, on the other hand, there is only a perception of less care, another strategy will be necessary. In that case, emotional support and conversations may be needed to help people realize the reality and overcome the false perception.

- Some members may be more emotionally stuck than others.

Within a congregation, some members will often be more closely connected to the pastor than others. The same may be true within the leadership community as well. The transitional leader should make sure that extra support is provided to those feeling the loss more deeply. Loss and grief can vary significantly from one member to another.

Ways to Provide Pastoral Care

There are multiple ways to provide pastoral care to the congregation and leaders during a transition. The transitional leader may use systems already in place or use methods unique to the season of transition. Which methods to use should be based on a careful assessment of needs.

- The transitional leader and other trained individuals can meet with people one-on-one.

Depending on the dynamics at play in the congregation, one-on-one visitation may be a practical and beneficial way to care for people. Interviews designed for information gathering can also be used as opportunities to provide pastoral care. Careful use of words in conversation can do much good and bring healing: "Rash language cuts and maims, but there is healing in the words of the wise." (Proverbs 12:18 TM)

- Leaders should practice therapeutic and attentive listening.

A wise man once said, "Learn to listen with three ears: listen to what people are saying, listen for what they are not saying, and listen for what people would like to say but can't put into words." During times of grief and loss, the transitional leader who listens deeply will often hear things people would like to say but can't put into words.

Attentive listening is not about listening to find a pathway forward as much as it is about listening so people feel heard and loved. As Paul Tillich wisely said, "The first duty of love is to listen."

- Leaders should be extra sensitive to people who may be in crisis.

When people are in a crisis situation, what do they appreciate from others? It is not advice they value or a rah-rah speech but a person simply being present with them in the crisis. It's the gifts of time, silence, empathy, and supportive prayer that matter.

> "To love someone deeply gives you strength. Being loved by someone deeply gives you courage."
> — Lao Tzu

It is also important to match the care with the need. People on the fringe of the loss may not be feeling the pastor's exit very deeply at all. They should be handled differently from those feeling the transition deeply.

- Provision must be made for visitation to the sick and needy.

If the congregation has a well organized system of visitation for the sick and needy, either by lay volunteers or by staff, this may not be a significant issue. However, if the senior pastor looked after this ministry or was the catalyst behind it, attention will need to be given to this area to make sure all the bases are covered.

This may be an opportunity to equip new people within the body for this ministry. The transitional leader may become involved in providing this ministry or only in helping to coordinate it with the transition team and other leaders.

- It is important to practice intercessory prayer.

The season of closure is a time for prayer. One important focus for prayer is the kind that intercedes with God on behalf of people in need of his help. In the words of J. Oswald Sanders, "Prayer influences men by influencing God to influence them. It is not the prayer that moves men, but the God to whom we pray."

Intercessory prayer is something the Holy Spirit does for Christians: "We do not know what we ought to pray for, but the Spirit himself intercedes for us through wordless groans." (Romans 8:26 NIV) Intercession is also something all Christians can participate in: "And pray in the Spirit on all occasions with all kinds of prayers and requests. With this in mind, be alert and always keep on praying for all the Lord's people." (Ephesians 6:18 NIV)

- It is important to provide appropriate counseling and support.

During a crisis transition or in situations where there has been trauma and deep hurt, professional counseling and other support may be required. Some congregations have direct access to these services, while others will need to go outside to find them.

Significant pain requires time and care to heal. Ministry leaders must partner with the Holy Spirit, who is the true healer. God revealed himself to Moses, saying, "I am God your healer." (Exodus 15:26 TM)

- Pastoral services such as weddings and funerals must also be provided.

If the previous pastor was the one people relied on to perform rites of passage such as weddings and funerals, someone needs to fill that gap. This can be part of the transitional leader's responsibility, or it can be assigned to other leaders. The key is for the transitional leader and the congregational leaders to talk through a strategy and know how these needs will be addressed.

Reflective Questions

❖ What are some ways you would assess the current reality in the area of pastoral care within a congregation?

❖ How is pastoral care different in the intentional interim model compared to the typical interim model?

❖ What do you see as your gifts in this area of transitional ministry?

Chapter 7

Facilitating Administration

A dministration is the "management of the affairs of an organization."[5] The church is an organism but also an organization, made up of people, programs, and plans, all needing structure and support. Facilitating the day-to-day administration of the congregation is an important aspect of transitional ministry.

Basic administration takes place while healthy change and transition are going on. It is closely linked to facilitating organizational health but has more to do with short-term ongoing ministry function than with the bigger picture. The week-to-week ministry must continue during a pastoral transition so the church doesn't lose ground and see normal ministry activities grind to a halt. Times of transition don't have to be accompanied by the loss of regular ministry activity. In fact, the time between pastors can be an opportunity to strengthen ministry, not just maintain it.

Challenges When Organizing Day-to-Day Ministry

Administration is all about working with people, who inevitably bring their emotions and current reality to the situation. When seeking to organize people and ministry, the transitional leader may encounter certain additional challenges present because of the pastoral transition.

Those challenges may include:
- **Weary people**

The pastor's exit may have required some members of the congregation to engage in a flurry of activities, leaving them exhausted and needing time to rest.
- **Grieving people**

People who are feeling the loss of their previous pastor may be emotionally spent and not in a frame of mind to carry out administrative tasks.
- **Angry people**

Not all pastoral exits are smooth, leaving people feeling warm and fuzzy. Sometimes unresolved conflict produces disharmony, resentment, bitterness, and anger. Morale may be low, and church management may be hindered by the conflict.
- **Missing people**

It is not unusual for people to leave after a pastoral exit. This places added stress on those left behind, and this requires sensitivity and wisdom to manage.
- **Relational stress**

If there was tension between the former pastor and key leaders, there will be a spillover effect, which may include damaged relationships. The effects of the tension may not be visible, but they will resurface eventually.
- **Vision vacuum**

If the vision for ministry resided primarily in the exiting pastor or if the church's vision is old and outdated, there will be a vision vacuum, which will affect day-to-day ministry.
- **Leadership vacuum**

Following a pastoral exit, there may be a critical shortage of workers and competent leaders to work with.
- **Planning vacuum**

There may or may not be a current ministry plan. If there isn't, a temporary plan may need to be created to provide some momentum and direction during the transition.

- **Organizational weakness**

There may be a lack of organization and impaired lines of communication, resulting in confusion around expectations and ministry responsibilities.

- **Staff needs**

In a multi-staff church, care and attention need to be given to assessing the level of health within the staff. If the staff are feeling hurt, discouraged, bitter, or angry, they need to be given help to move to a place where ministry can function in a healthy way.

- **Sabbath mentality**

The entire congregation may be looking for a *sabbatical* break from ministry, a time to catch their breath and rest.

Developing an Administrative Pathway

In spite of the possible challenges, the role of those who are facilitating the transition is to breathe hope into the congregation and point the way forward. True hope is not wishful thinking but a bundle of expectations with a pathway to get there.

> "Hope prevents us from clinging to what we have and frees us to move away from the safe place and enter unknown and fearful territory."
> — Henri Nouwen

Administration is a way to engage Christ-followers with the mission and purpose of the church, to help them to see that ministry gaps and challenges are opportunities in disguise.

There are six stepping S.T.O.N.E.S. to consider when facilitating administration. This chapter discusses administration as it relates to the day-to-day ministry, but it should be kept in mind that administration needs to also connect to the bigger transitional blueprint. For more on the transitional blueprint, see Section 5 of this book.

The six stepping S.T.O.N.E.S. of facilitating administration are:

1. Scan the horizon.

Transitional leaders can't address what they don't first assess. Organizing day-to-day ministry begins with getting a clear picture of what is going on. This includes answering questions such as: "How well is ministry organized? What is the ministry plan? Who is doing what? What are the pressure points? What is missing?"

There is definite overlap when assessing a congregation in transition. The goal is to dig deep enough and gather data broadly enough to get a clear picture of what is going on in the congregation. Only with that information in hand is it possible to move to the next stepping stone.

2. Translate the findings into priorities.

Once the assessment has been done, the findings must be translated into priorities. This involves interpreting the data and answering the questions: "What does this mean? What do we need to do now based on what we see?"

Translating the findings is the job of leadership. This might include the transitional leader, the transition team, staff members, and others who will be responsible to implement what is planned.

3. Organize the priorities into a plan.

Day-to-day ministry priorities now need to be turned into a workable plan. This is the stepping stone that puts shoe leather to what has been discussed and what has been decided to be necessary.

More information on planning is found in Section 5 of this book. The reason it is included here is that planning ongoing ministry needs to be done as well as planning the bigger picture. Bobb Biehl asks a great planning question: "What are the three things we can do in the next 90 days that would make a 50 percent difference?"

4. Negotiate the distribution of the ministry.

Once the needs have been assessed and a plan is in place, what is needed next is people to carry out the plan. One of the best illustrations of how to organize work through people is Jethro's advice to his son-in-law, Moses. Moses was wearing himself out by doing all the work himself, and he needed to learn to delegate:

Moses listened to the counsel of his father-in-law and did everything he said. Moses picked competent men from all Israel and set them as leaders over the people who were organized by the thousand, by the hundred, by fifty, and by ten. They took over the everyday work... (Exodus 18:24-26 TM)

Facilitating administration is learning to work through people to accomplish the work God wants done.

5. Equip and supervise those who serve.

A word of caution is in order when delegating ministry to others: those involved in the work need to be equipped and supervised. The adage "orient, involve, equip" is a good ministry model.

J. Oswald Sanders defines leadership as "the ability to recognize the special abilities and limitations of others, combined with the capacity to fit each one into the job where he will do his best."[6]

Maturity in the body comes from involving every part of the body and equipping those workers through training, support, and feedback. Paul's words to the Ephesians describe how gifted leaders are to equip others to do the work, not just dump ministry responsibility on the untrained and ill-equipped:

So Christ himself gave the apostles, the prophets, the evangelists, the pastors and teachers, to equip his people for works of service, so that the body of Christ may be built up until we all reach unity in the faith and in the knowledge of the Son of God and become mature, attaining to the whole measure of the fullness of Christ. (Ephesians 4:11-13 NIV)

6. Shape communication.

A critical part of managing the affairs of a congregation is to shape the flow of communication. Leaders communicating with the congregation and the congregation communicating with leadership is like oil in an engine. It reduces friction and helps the parts work well together.

Clear communication is about developing systems and methods that keep the channels of information open. Healthy communication helps contain bad gossip, lowers uncertainty, allows people to feel heard, and facilitates the change process. The key is to communicate information that is group specific (telling the congregation, the staff, ministry leaders, the board, etc. what they specifically need to know) without breaking confidentiality or going outside predetermined communication policies.

Reflective Questions

❖ What are some ways you would assess the current administrative and management structures of a congregation?

❖ How is administration different in the intentional transitional model compared to the typical or traditional approach to interim ministry?

❖ What are your strengths in the area of administration?

Chapter 8

Facilitating Relationship Renewal

A t the heart of transitional ministry is the condition of the corporate soul of the congregation. The main goal of any transitional ministry is to prepare the congregation for the healthy entrance of the next senior pastor by creating an environment of joy and peace. This preparation includes giving attention to the relational condition of the congregation. The relational condition is often evident in the way a congregation prays and plays together. The congregation's spiritual life, body life, and community engagement are all indicators of its soul condition.

Defining Relationship Renewal

Relationship renewal refers to the connection members of a congregation have with God (upward), the connection they have with one another (inward), and the ability they have to connect with people around them (outward). All three aspects are interdependent and require equal attention during the transitional process.

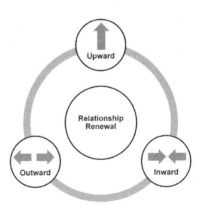

Figure 5: Three Aspects of Relationship Renewal

Mike Breen, in his book *Building a Discipling Culture*, describes Jesus as embodying all three aspects in his life and ministry:

> Jesus lived a three-dimensional life. First, he did nothing apart from his Father. He called a team of people together to be his friends in the kingdom community he was building. Having communicated with the Father (Up) and gathered these friends (In), Jesus then moved (Out) into the crowd and did the work of the kingdom — proclaiming the Good News, challenging injustice, teaching the people, healing the sick, and revealing the love of the Father to the world.[7]

When a congregation works on all three aspects (upward, inward, and outward) of relationship renewal, genuine *shalom* (peace) occurs. *Shalom* is "the lack of disharmony or agitation and the presence of wholeness or completeness." *Shalom* is not the absence of differences or conflict in a congregation but the ability to manage and address conflict with *agape* love.

Foundational Principles for Relationship Renewal

1.   Relationship Renewal is Built on the *Agape* Principle.

The *agape* principle recognizes that God's purpose for all members of a congregation is that they enjoy a wholesome (*shalom*) relationship with God and with one another. In light of the *agape* principle, every effort must be made to heal broken relationships and develop relationships reflecting the one enjoyed by the Father, Son, and Holy Spirit.

Doug Harris describes the *agape* principle this way:

> It is conformity to the *agape* principle that is the secret of conflict resolution, relationship renewal and connectedness among people on this earth. *Agape* is the golden key that opens every door. It is the pathway to resolving all issues, resolving all problems and making possible the experiencing of heavenly interpersonal relationships on earth at this time. It is the secret of

experiencing unity in the church. Only as church members reflect the characteristics of our Lord's *agape*, will the prayer of our Lord be answered — that the connections and relationships among the body would reflect the connection and relationship enjoyed by God the Father and God the Son. The *agape* principle validates our claim to be Christians, i.e., followers or disciples of our Lord. We have no claim to the designation as a church of the living God if the relationship among the members is not an expression of the *agape* principle.

The *agape* principle cements connections and strengthens relationships. It is the basis for resolving all church conflict, restoring connections and renewing relationships. Conflicts, disputes and broken relationships are the wounds inflicted upon congregations when they live by the *eros* principle. Resolution, healing and harmony are the results of living by the *agape* principle.[8]

Jesus' commandment to love supports the premise that without *agape* love, relationship renewal is impossible. Love affects all three aspects (upward, inward, and outward) of who a congregation is, what it does, and why it exists as the church. The command to love was Jesus' response to the teachers of the law who asked him for his kingdom priorities:

> "This is the secret of life: the self lives only by dying, finds its identity (and its happiness) only by self-forgetfulness, self-giving, self-sacrifice, and agape love."
> — Peter Kreeft

"Of all the commandments, which is the most important?" "The most important one," answered Jesus, "is this: 'Hear, O Israel: The Lord our God, the Lord is one. Love the Lord your God with all your heart and with all your soul and with all your mind and with all your strength.' The second is this: 'Love your neighbor as yourself.' There is no commandment greater than these." (Mark 12:28-31 NIV)

2. Relationship Renewal Makes the Gospel Central.

Definitions of "gospel" abound. J.I. Packer defines "gospel" as "God saves sinners." A broader definition of "gospel" encompasses both the God-Man-Christ-Response perspective and the Creation-Fall-Redemption-Restoration perspective. Ed Stetzer presents a definition that is broad enough to include the depth and width of the work God is up to in the world:

> The objective of a transitional leader is to help refocus the congregation towards the goal of the gospel — to produce mature followers of Christ.

> The gospel is the good news that God, who is more holy than we can imagine, looked upon with compassion, people, who are more sinful than we would possibly admit, and sent Jesus into history to establish His Kingdom and reconcile people and the world to Himself. Jesus, whose love is more extravagant than we can measure, came to sacrificially die for us so that, by His death and resurrection, we might gain through His grace what the Bible defines as new and eternal life.[9]

A congregation can easily get distracted from the importance of partnering with God to proclaim the good news to the world. The distractions can include unfocused traditions, mismanaged organizational systems, unresolved personal conflicts, limited resources, abundant resources, and a focus on programs rather than people.

Relationship renewal involves restoring the gospel to the central and primary place. The objective of a transitional leader is to help members of the congregation refocus on the gospel and live fully committed, Christ-centered lives.

3. Relationship Renewal Is all about Disciple-making.

The goal of the Christian life is to become like Christ and reach full maturity as his follower. Anything short of this goal is unfaithful to the Bible's message. Relationship renewal is about facilitating growth towards maturity. Paul wrote about this to the church at Ephesus:

It was he who gave some to be apostles, some to be prophets, some to be evangelists, and some to be pastors and teachers, to prepare God's people for works of service, so that the body of Christ may be built up until we all reach unity in the faith and in the knowledge of the Son of God and become mature, attaining to the whole measure of the fullness of Christ. (Ephesians 4:11-13 NIV)

Dallas Willard, in the book *Renovation of the Heart*, reflects on Paul's words to the Ephesians:

What we see here is not an impossible dream, a hopeless idealization. It has been done and can be done now, if we turn our efforts under God in the right direction. And that direction would be one that makes spiritual formation in Christ-likeness the exclusive primary goal of the local congregation. This is what one would naturally expect after having read what Paul says—and, indeed, after having read what Jesus sent his world revolutionaries out to do (Matthew 28:18-20).[10]

Mature disciples are engaged in all three aspects of relationship renewal. They are upwardly established in God, inwardly connected to the body, and outwardly relating to those not yet following Jesus.

4. Relationship Renewal Puts a Fresh Focus on Evangelism.

Relationship renewal will help members of the congregation rediscover Jesus' passion to pass on the message of his love to those who have not yet experienced it. Many churches need to rediscover what it means to be incarnational[11] in their witness instead of expecting that church events will be enough to help people connect to God.

Contexts will vary, but there is a common theme emerging in how today's nonbeliever crosses the great divide and discovers the life-changing love of Christ. Mike Breen summarizes the shift this way:

> Today we have a generation of nonbelievers that might not ever enter the doors of a church unless they have already had a positive encounter with a Christian in the world. The idea of evangelism frightens many Christians. They rarely see outreach modeled in a way that they feel capable of doing. That is why their evangelistic efforts are usually confined to bringing a friend or colleague to church in the hope that a professional Christian will share the Gospel with them. But once Jesus' strategy of outward relationships is explained, that fear often vanishes. When they are encouraged to look for people they naturally connect with and build relationships with them, sharing the Gospel message seems much more possible.[12]

The time between pastors does not need to be a time to ignore intentional evangelism. On the contrary, a time of transition can be an opportunity to fan the flame of a congregation's witness. It can be a time to challenge disciples to outwardly focus their *agape* love towards friends and neighbors who do not yet know Jesus personally.

Elements for Facilitating Relationship Renewal

Facilitating effective relationship renewal involves a number of elements. It starts with the transitional leader and the leadership community modeling a heart of *agape* love. It then moves into laying out a pathway the congregation can follow to get from where they are (here) to where God wants them to be (there) in their relationships.

The transitional leader should work with the congregation and its leadership to map out a pathway for relationship renewal both by teaching and by showing how it is done. As leaders practice relationship renewal in their own

"You teach what you know but you reproduce who you are."
— John Maxwell

lives and ministries, they are better able to facilitate relationship renewal in the congregation.

There are five elements to consider when facilitating relationship renewal:

1. Assess and make ongoing observations.

Assessing the corporate soul is done by using both Holy Spirit-guided intuition and tangible tools and data-gathering methods. Some relationship health issues will be readily noticeable as the transitional leader observes congregational behaviors. Deeper realities will be discovered as the leader hears from people in one-to-one dialogue or digs deeper into the hidden areas of congregational life.

It's important to cast the net of observation broadly in assessing relational health. When a congregation of 100 sits far apart from each other in an auditorium seating 500, it says something about *inward* relational health. The tone around the board table says something about the *inward* relational health of the leaders. The way people speak of their walk with God and who they are experiencing God to be speaks to their *upward* relational health. The reputation of the congregation in the community speaks to *outward* relational health.

Diagnostic tools abound and should be selected and used very carefully. For the best outcome, it's wise to use a collaborative discernment process once the data has been collected. That could include facilitated conversations about the data and guided conversations about what should be done as a result of what has been learned. It's not enough to have an expert collect data and give an interpretation, and then expect change will result from that.

What is learned by assessment and observation will help the transitional leader and transition team develop a pathway towards healing, recovery, and health. Healthy congregational living can be celebrated, while areas of relationship weakness can be worked on.

2. Use a systems approach to strengthening relationships.

It's important to adopt a systems approach when working with congregations. This approach assumes that the behavior that is seen at any given point in time is connected to something greater. The parts are connected to the whole. When a congregation is understood to be an interconnected system, it is easy to see the relatedness of the parts to the whole.

> "In a systems approach we look beyond the trees and see the forest."
> — Peter Steinke

Systems thinking adds a valuable perspective when working towards greater relationship health. Peter L. Steinke makes a case for a systems approach with these words:

> Systems thinking deepens our understanding of life. We see it as a rich complexity of interdependent parts. Basically, a system is a set of forces and events that interact, such as a weather system or the solar system. To think systemically is to look at the ongoing, vital interaction of the connected parts.[13]

Systems thinking stands back and looks at the whole congregational story with its many chapters, themes, and seasons. When a problem appears, the transitional pastor must not look at it in isolation from the whole but look for the connections to other contributing factors.

Systems thinking looks at what is happening within the family units of the congregation. It takes note of the history, losses, and turning points of the congregational story. What is learned from the whole will have an impact on decision making and will guide what conversations need to be facilitated.

> "Systems thinking is a discipline for seeing wholes. It is a framework for seeing interrelationships rather than things, for seeing patterns of change rather than static 'snapshots.'" — Peter Senge

For instance, through extensive digging, the transitional leader might discover that the controlling and dominating board member will not forgive his brother-in-law, who also sits on the board. Through a hallway conversation, the transitional leader might find out that the associate pastor was relieved and excited when the previous pastor left because he has wanted his job for a while now. The individual parts affect the whole!

3. Design a collaborative pathway for renewal.

After a clear picture has been gained of the heart and soul of the congregation and a systems lens has been applied to the evaluation, it will be time to develop a collaborative plan. The developers of the plan will include the transitional leader and the transition team, in partnership with the leadership (i.e., board, staff, elders, and outside leaders).

The time required and the intensity of the focus on relationship renewal will vary from situation to situation. In some congregations, relationship renewal will require vigilant monitoring due to deep woundedness. In others, relationships may be strong, and less attention may be required. In either case, the transitional leader often takes on the supervisory responsibility in this area, keeping in touch with where things are at and what needs to be done next.

One effective way to design a collaborative pathway is to use process thinking. Process thinking asks three basic questions: What? So What? Now What?

- **The "What?"** describes the framework of the conversation. It asks, "What are we talking about, what are we trying to solve, and what needs attention?"
- **The "So What?"** describes the meaning and relevance of the issue to those affected by it. It asks, "So what does it matter to us in this situation?"

> Process Thinking:
> What?
> So What?
> Now What?

- **The "Now What?"** focuses on what will be done with what is discovered in the conversations. It asks, "Now what will we do about this issue?"

73

Process thinking can be done in small or large groups and is useful for creating a collaborative conversation around a hot topic. It helps define a topic, clarifies the group's perspective on the topic, and provides an opportunity for creative and cooperative thinking about what can be done.

4. Ensure implementation and ongoing accountability.

Once sufficient information has been gathered, systems thinking has been applied, and a suitable pathway has been developed, it's time to implement the plan and track the progress.

There is no rule saying only one team or group will do all the work. It's wise to divide the work among teams or cluster groups who will focus on the various areas of relationship renewal— upward, inward, and outward. The more people involved and personally responsible for the outcomes, the higher the potential for achieving successful outcomes.

A critical question needing an answer at some point is: "How will we know we are healthy enough to move to the next phase of the transitional process?" In other words, how can progress in the area of relationship renewal be measured? It's a great question but one not easy to answer.

What makes answering the question of "healthy enough" difficult is the way words mean different things to different people. The best approach is to agree on a definition of "healthy enough" early on in the process. Questions such as the ones in Chapter 25 may be helpful in this regard.

5. Provide coaching for positional and functional leaders.

A transitional leader's best avenue for influencing a congregation in the area of relationship renewal is through coaching and encouraging the congregation's positional and functional leaders. Positional leaders have an official leadership or ministry responsibility but may or may not be functional, healthy, or spiritually mature. Functional leaders may or may not have a position of responsibility, but they influence congregational health. Both types of leaders require attention and support in this area.

The leaders of the congregation are the immune system for the body. Peter L. Steinke says of congregational leaders: "They are positioned to be the church family's 'differentiation,' the immune cells of the whole. They are the body's mature cells...responsible for defining themselves and ensuring the group's definition of who they are."[14]

If leaders are healthy, involved, and maturing disciples, they will provide a strong impetus for relationship renewal. Transitional leaders should support, pray for, and challenge the leaders in their upward relationship with God, their inward relationship with the body, and their outward connection with those not yet following Jesus.

Adequate assessment, systems thinking, wise planning, thorough follow-through, and attentive coaching will increase the chances of achieving relationship renewal. The result will be a healthier body functioning as Jesus intended it to function.

Reflective Questions

❖ What stories, concepts, or images come to mind as you consider facilitating relationship renewal with a congregation you are working with?

❖ What blocks or hinders relationship renewal from happening?

❖ What are the critical character qualities needed in a transitional leader to help facilitate relationship renewal?

Deep-seated Renewal and the Cross

The chairs in the room were set up in a circle around a fifteen-foot wooden cross. The transition team had set aside two hours for a "Prayer and Repentance Assembly" and asked several people to read relevant Scriptures moving from confession towards forgiveness. Three times the expected number of people showed up. One person wept the whole time. Others spent time on their knees.

There was a large pile of rocks on the platform from a previous sermon illustration. At a very deep moment in the evening, someone took a rock from the pile, spoke about how his personal sin had caused pain in the congregation, asked for forgiveness, and placed the rock at the base of the wooden cross. The room responded with quiet words of forgiveness. A trend was started.

Several others grabbed rocks, stated something quietly towards the cross or openly to the others in the room, and placed the rock at the base of the cross. Several people began to cross the room and have quiet conversations with others, ending in hugs or prayers.

What had prompted this evening was a deep congregational assessment. The assessment had uncovered injured hearts over the way the congregation had managed a leadership transition ten months earlier. Relationships had been broken. Spiritual life with God had been interrupted.

The transition team, under the guidance of the transitional leader, had discerned that the newly developed transitional blueprint had to start with relationship renewal. There was a clear acknowledgement that renewal of this kind could not be forced or manipulated. It had to be God inspired. The task of the transition team had been to create a safe and focused environment. The evening gave the congregation an opportunity to meet with God and each other around Scriptures and songs pertaining to prayer and repentance. God favored their efforts. Christ was honored.

Not everyone in the congregation was able to participate in the "Prayer and Repentance Assembly," and not everyone wanted to. No guilt or shame was placed on anyone who did not attend. There was a seepage of life from that one evening that had a lingering affect on everyone. It resulted in a congregation ready to move forward together into God's heart for the community.

— Alan Simpson

A Divided Church Unites

Ten years ago, this badly fragmented church had lost its lead pastor. The members had quarreled over whether to have multiple services, had quarreled over "who was in charge," had developed a dislike for the youth pastor, and had become angry about the worship style. The church was situated in a growing suburb of a large Canadian city and had a very desirable location. But in the middle of this great opportunity, the church members were preoccupied with matters of personal preference and issues of control. Lost people were hardly a blip on their radar.

There were three leadership bodies continually clashing, plus a group of seniors incessantly carping. In desperation, the members of the congregation invited an interim pastor to lead them in rethinking their reason for existence. They began by honestly facing their past.

The congregation constructed a large history wall and began to process it. The story literally brought the members of the congregation to tears as they saw their behavior in all its ugliness — their self-centeredness, intolerance, and unwillingness to forgive — and finally dealt with it.

The youth pastor asked forgiveness from the church for his behavior. The church leaders asked forgiveness from the youth pastor for their lack of tolerance and support. People owned their own baggage and began asking and receiving forgiveness from each other.

With relationships under repair, the church began to look forward. The members began to see the families in their neighborhood. They became aware of the personal contacts and friends they had. They began to see the tremendous need of the hungry and homeless in their city's downtown core.

With the members of the congregation seeing with new eyes, a vision greater than themselves emerged. Reaching families became the heart of the church's ministry, but the homeless and hungry were not forgotten either. It did take time—even after forgiveness, the members had to learn to let go and love each other—but they were committed to the process.

The congregation also reorganized its governance structures and gave control to the leaders. The members had to let go of their preferences. Today, several years later, the church has more than doubled in size, and the vision has become a reality. That congregation has spearheaded a ministry to the homeless which has galvanized the churches of the community to action and unity. The church's two services are filled with young families; many of the new members didn't know Christ a few years ago. The church's leadership is united, and baptisms are a regular occurrence.

The vision the members of this congregation saw is being realized and continues to emerge. Convinced that God is doing a new thing, they want to discern together what the next chapter might look like. They are not the same people!

– Dave Jackson

Chapter 9

Facilitating Vision Clarity

A healthy congregation has a God-sized vision uniquely suited to its context and cultural setting. The time between pastors is an opportunity for a congregation to take a fresh look at its vision and, if necessary, renew or redo its vision.

The vision-clarifying process involves guided conversations with the leaders and members of the congregation about what is and what could be. If the vision is seen to be relevant and clear, the time of pastoral transition can be an opportunity to implement the vision in every corner of congregational life. If the vision is found to be lacking, the time of transition can be a time to begin the process of determining a new vision.

This chapter examines four organizing principles for clarifying vision and ten guiding principles that give structure to a vision-clarifying process.

Four Organizing Principles to Hold in Tension

There are four organizing principles or qualities of a congregation that it needs to hold in tension as it develops and implements a God-sized vision. These four principles reflect the "synergistic" nature of congregational life—how various aspects must work together in order for there to be health and life. These four organizing principles are presented in George Bullard's book *FaithSoaring Churches*. They are visionary leadership, relationship experiences, programs, and accountable management. These principles correspond to what Jesus stated in Mark's Gospel:

And you shall love the Lord your God with all your heart, and with all your soul, and with all your mind, and with all your strength. (Mark 12:30 NASB)

Vision is about heart. Relationships are about soul. Programs are about mind. Management is about strength.

Visionary leadership produces a congregation that has a strong, clear, and passionate sense of its identity, its mission, its purpose, its core values, and its spiritual journey. Such a congregation knows who it is, what it values, what it believes, where it is headed, and how it is going to get there.

Relationship experiences include evangelism, new member recruitment, assimilation, fellowship, spiritual growth, discipleship development, and mobilization of church members to serve. This covers the whole process through which those not yet following Jesus become devoted Christ-followers. It is about how people relate to God, to one another, and to the community in which they live.

Programs are the framework through which the church members can have the best possible relationship experiences with God, one another, and the surrounding community. Programs are a means to the desired end and not the end themselves. Programs must deepen and enhance relationships.

Accountable management supports the vision. It pulls together the various resources of the congregation. It is made up of the formal and informal governance and decision-making structures, the traditions and culture of the congregation, and the readiness of the congregation for change and growth. It provides a basis for deciding how the people, finances, facilities, equipment, and material resources of the congregation are used.

Vision, relationships, programs, and management individually are not enough. They must work together—*become synergistic*—in order for a congregation to reach its faith potential. The analogy of seats in a car is a helpful picture of how they interact with one another. Vision is driving, while relationships help navigate. Programs are in the back seat behind relationships, providing the framework of ministries and activities within which relationships can flourish. Management is in the back seat behind vision, providing the administrative infrastructure to allow vision to catch the wind of God's Spirit.

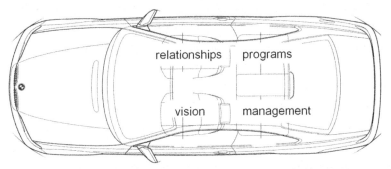

Figure 6: Four Organizing Principles

Ten Principles Pauing the Way for Vision Clarity

Here are ten principles that are useful for guiding the vision-clarifying process. These principles do not provide everything needed for a vision-clarifying process, but they do provide a framework and point towards other helpful resources. The underlying assumption is that the transitional leader will find the right approach to match his or her particular situation or will be able to use the following principles to customize an approach best suited to the context and culture.

Principle 1: Clarifying Vision Requires Accurate Assessment.

Assessment is a biblical idea. The men of Issachar, who fought for David, were commended because they "understood the times and knew what Israel should do." (1 Chronicles 12:32 NIV) Solomon believed in assessing a situation before acting: "Don't jump to conclusions—there may be a perfectly good explanation for what you just saw." (Proverbs 25:8 TM)

Assessment is comparable to what a family doctor does when a patient comes in for a check-up. Before prescribing medicine or treatment, he puts the patient through a battery of tests to get a clear picture of what is going on. Congregations are guilty at times of changing programs, policies, and personnel before they have even asked the question, "What is really going on here?"

Assessment is the process of stepping back before stepping ahead. It is figuring out where "here" is before having a conversation about "there." There are numerous tools that can be used for assessment. Below are a few examples the transitional leader should add to his or her toolbox and have available for the right situation.

Example 1: S.W.O.T. Analysis

The S.W.O.T. analysis is a tool to look at a congregation's Strengths, Weaknesses, Opportunities, and Threats and to have a conversation about what is really going on. The information gleaned can be useful and can feed into further conversations about where the congregation might want to go in the future. The S.W.O.T. analysis diagram pictured here can serve as a template for writing down the information gathered. The diagram

Strengths	Weaknesses
Opportunities	Threats

Figure 7: SWOT Analysis

can be put on a large piece of paper for a large group or on a note pad for a few leaders around a table.

Example 2: Forums and Interviews

Group forums and one-on-one interviews are excellent ways to gather helpful feedback and information about congregational life. Forums and interviews can serve multiple purposes because they not only provide valuable information, but also give people an opportunity to be heard and to hear what other people are sensing and saying.

A group forum could consider questions such as:

- How is God speaking to us as a body through Scripture?
- What common themes do these Scriptures suggest?
- What values are important around here?
- How well are we practicing these values?
- How might we as individuals be contributing to any deficiencies within our community?
- What are the top needs, problems, or issues we need to address?

An individual interview could include the following questions:

- If I moved into this area, would you invite me to this church? If yes, why should I come?
- What makes this church unique or special among others in the area?
- What is the greatest strength of this church? Why?
- What is the greatest weakness or challenge of this church?
- What is the vision or direction of this church?
- What are the most urgent issues this transition must address?

Example 3: Life Cycle[15]

Every congregation has a life cycle. Determining where a congregation is in its life cycle can be helpful because it provides a realistic context within which to clarify its vision.

Two questions to ask when considering the life cycle are:
- Where would you place our congregation on the life cycle? Why?
- What might this mean in terms of the approach we should take in our planning?

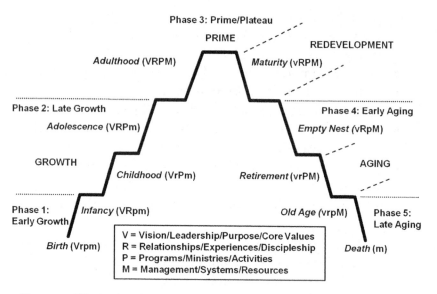

Figure 8: Life Cycle with Developmental Stages and Organizing Principles

Example 4: Health Assessments and Surveys

Well designed surveys with good questions can be useful to assess congregational health. The key to conducting a survey is not to simply *do one* but to *guide a conversation about the survey* and what it means after it is done.

Some questions to ask in a congregational survey:
- How would you describe the level of spiritual maturity in our congregation?

84

- How are we developing new leaders? Describe the process.
- How would you describe the overall strength of our volunteers?
- When you think of our leaders, what words would you use to describe them?
- How would you describe the overall morale of our church?
- How would you describe your own personal mission?
- Do you enthusiastically invite others to worship with us?

Remember: the value of any survey is not in the data that is collected but in the conversations about the data. Those conversations can lead to greater awareness and clarity about the way things really are, based on people's perspectives and experiences. The next step is to facilitate follow-up conversations about where God wants the congregation to go and about what needs changing in order for the congregation to get there.

Principle 2: Connection with God Fuels Vision Clarification.

Prayer, connecting intentionally with God, creates an environment in which a healthy transition can take place. It is the heart and soul of relationship renewal between God and the congregation, but is also instrumental in the process of clarifying vision.

Planning and clarifying vision will be shortsighted and based solely on the wisdom of people if a strong connection with God, his Word, and his Spirit isn't central to the conversation. What matters is not *how* the congregation practices prayer but *that* it practices prayer.

A helpful prayer and discernment framework for discovering a God-sized vision is found in Henry Blackaby's book *Experiencing God*. He suggests seven realities which are important to keep in mind:

1. God is always at work around you.

2. God pursues a continuing love relationship with you that is real and personal.

3. God invites you to become involved with Him in His work.

4. God speaks by the Holy Spirit through the Bible, prayer, circumstances, and the church to reveal Himself, His purposes, and His ways.

5. God's invitation for you to work with Him always leads you to a crisis of belief that requires faith and action.

6. You must make major adjustments in your life to join God in what He is doing.

7. You come to know God by experience as you obey Him and He accomplishes His work through you.[16]

The vision-clarifying process will progress as the congregation's members are mobilized to seek God, see what he is doing, and adjust their lives to what he is doing. It is, after all, the Holy Spirit who should serve as the leader in any vision-clarifying process.

Principle 3: Clarifying Vision Requires a Planning Road Map.

There are certain steps in the vision-clarifying process that are fairly consistent among the various methods used in congregational planning. The following road map identifies four phases to the vision-clarifying process. These phases are broadly transferable regardless of the context.

This road map provides guidelines for mapping out a process but allows for the use of various tools and methods for each step. It is built on the foundation of congregational ownership of the process and a guiding team with enough influence within the

86

congregation to keep the process moving through the ups and downs.

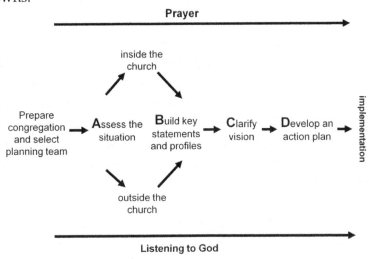

Figure 9: Vision Planning Road Map

The four phases of the vision-clarifying process are:

1. Assess the situation.

During this phase, the goal is to gather information from both inside and outside the congregation, to develop a clear, up-to-date snapshot of the congregation and of the surrounding community. This information can be gathered in a concentrated process, or the process can be spread out over a number of days or weeks. How and when the data is gathered will depend on the leadership's sense of urgency.

It should be kept in mind that the data gathered during this phase of the vision-clarifying process will have a much broader use. It will not only help produce the key statements and profiles (discussed in phase two), but will also be useful when writing the documents that guide the search for a new pastor.

2. Build key statements and profiles.

The second phase involves turning ideas and data into understandable documents. There are basically three types of written documents to prepare in this phase of the vision-clarifying process. The first is a local church profile, which is a clear picture of the current congregation. The second document is a community profile, describing the greater community within which the congregation exists and which it is called to minister to. This includes demographics, cultural dynamics, and any other information pertinent to shaping future ministry. The third document describes the core values and purpose of the congregation.

Core values are those preferences, assumptions, and unique characteristics God has built into the fabric of a congregation. They are the *valuables* a congregation is willing to sacrifice for and is able to use to drive ministry. Adjusting the values or introducing new values takes a great deal of work and intentionality but is necessary if deep change is to stick. A congregation's purpose is the biblical mandate God has given his church, expressed in words and language fitting the particular congregation's context. Purpose tends to be more general in nature, while vision is more unique.

3. Clarify the vision.

The process of discovering God's vision for the congregation is a journey including prayer, listening, holy conversations, dream sessions, times in God's Word, and interaction with the information gathered during the assessment phase of this process. The end result is a statement describing the vision God has revealed to the congregation. It may be longer or shorter, depending on the particular vision. A metaphor or slogan may be chosen to help capture and communicate the vision.

What exactly is a vision? George Bullard offers a helpful perspective:

We need to remember that vision is not a fifteen word or less statement crafted in a back room by a committee, printed on the worship folder, memorized, and then recited on cue. That is a vision statement. Any similarity between a vision statement and true vision is purely accidental. Vision is a movement of God that is memorable rather than a statement of humankind that is memorized. We cast and cast vision until we are captivated by it.

Developing a vision statement is not a difficult task. Becoming captivated by that vision is the hard part. Believing the vision is God pulling the congregation forward into the future rather than simply an organizational prediction of the future. Consistently living into the vision is the hard part.[17]

4. Develop an action plan.

An action plan summarizes the vision in clearly stated goals, accompanied by action steps, completion dates, and the names of the people responsible to make sure everything gets done. The action plan provides the road map and timetable for moving the church into the future.

Action planning requires continual review and evaluation to be effective. Far too many action plans are developed but then sit on the shelf, never fully implemented. The key to implementation is to make the plan easy enough to understand; it should be tied to the congregation's values, purpose, and vision and broken down into bite-sized pieces. Tackling an action plan is a little like eating an elephant—there is only one way to do that: one bite at a time.

The plan must become part of meeting agendas and integrated into the feedback loop to make sure that what is being done is what the plan says should be done. Programs, activities, and structures must be aligned with the plan so energy isn't lost on secondary pursuits.

There are several other vision and ministry planning methods and processes available. Here is a list of some of the resources available for helping to clarify vision and facilitate ministry planning:

- Appreciative Inquiry[18]
- Aubrey Malphurs Consulting[19]
- The Columbia Partnership — Transforming Congregations[20]
- Masterplanning by Bobb Biehl[21]
- Natural Church Development[22]
- Refocusing Your Church: Church Resource Ministries[23]
- Sonlife Ministries[24]

Principle 4: Clarifying Vision Requires an Awareness of the Change Process.

A proper understanding of the change process is essential when facilitating a vision-clarifying process. The reason for this is that any attempt to change vision and direction will face resistance. People are being asked to leave their comfort zones and the places where they have made big investments in order to move to unfamiliar territory; they need to be convinced that the new destination is better.

Loren Mead, in his book *A Change of Pastors,* refers to a study by behavioral scientist Kurt Lewin:

> Lewin made the point that the problem with human institutions is their very homeostasis. He noted that organizations are always stable because they are a balance of opposing forces held together, frozen in equilibrium, and they cannot change until that equilibrium is somehow broken. He stated a very simple prescription of three steps that had to be taken if one wanted to see change happen: 1) the frozen equilibrium had to be unfrozen; 2) the desired change had to be installed; and 3) the organism/ organization then had to be refrozen with the change in place.[25]

Mead goes on to say that when pastors leave, it is a moment of unfreezing. It is a moment when the forces holding the congregation immovable are loosened. It is a time when the status quo can be questioned and explored without people feeling violated.

The skill set required to go from *unfreeze* to *change* to *refreeze* is the ability to lead the change process. The process of clarifying the vision includes tampering with "the way we do things around here."

Principle 5: The Right People Must Be Involved in Clarifying Vision.

Who are the right people? The answer will depend on the congregation's leadership culture and what is believed regarding *where vision comes from*. There are four approaches to determining where vision comes from. They are:

1. The congregation comes up with the vision.

This approach says, "Authentic vision for our congregation can only originate in the membership."[26] Any proposal for the future will be brought to the congregation for ratification to ensure it truly represents the people.

2. The pastor brings the vision to the congregation.

This approach says, "Our ordained minister is our spiritual leader. As a person of prayer, our pastor spends time discerning God's intentions for this church. Through preaching, teaching, and organizational leadership, our pastor offers the congregation a unifying vision for the future and invites other leaders to participate in bringing that vision to fruition."[27]

3. The denomination provides the congregational vision.

This approach says, "The primary unit of mission is not the congregation, but rather the wider fellowship of believers in this region."[28] In this approach, the denomination is instrumental in setting congregational vision, inspiring and guiding the process through regional goals held up as benchmarks for the congregations in that region.

4. Vision emerges as we make meaning together.

This view values a collaborative approach to arriving at vision, deciding together "what is, what's important, and what God is saying to us."[29] A team approach to vision clarification underlines the value of hearing from all perspectives. It values the perspectives of the congregation, the pastor, the congregational leadership, and the denomination.

This approach involves the greatest number of people in the vision-clarifying process, and this has real value. Each approach may be appropriate in certain situations, but generally the more people involved in the conversation, the greater the engagement when it comes time to turn the vision into action.

Principle 6: Agreeing on Definitions Impacts Vision Clarification.

One place where vision and ministry planning get stuck is words and their meaning. The words used to describe a vision may not mean the same thing to the various people sitting around the table. People come from a variety of backgrounds and have unique perspectives on the words they like to use.

The words needing definition and agreement include: vision, mission, purpose, values, goals, priorities, action steps, strategic initiatives, key result areas (KRAs), and sub-goals. There are as many different ways to use these words as there are congregations.

What really matters when it comes to words and definitions? Not the words themselves, but the ability to arrive at a clear and specific future together. In other words, it is essential to both pick the words and agree on what those words will mean in this particular context.

When it comes to agreement on the terms to use, it is important to keep the bigger picture in mind. The focus should remain on where the congregation is going and what it hopes to achieve. The definitions accompanying the words should describe the uniqueness of the congregation. The words must be clear, providing a pathway people can follow for moving forward and a blueprint people can use for taking action.

Principle 7: Clarifying Vision Taps into Factors Motivating Change.

Motivation is an inside job. It's not a matter of bringing in external motivation but finding a way to tap into the motivation already present. In the words of Stephen Covey, "Motivation is a fire from within. If someone else tries to light that fire under you, chances are it will burn very briefly."

There are three factors that will effectively spur congregational motivation, giving energy to the vision-clarifying process:

1. Pain

When people hurt enough, they are more likely to consider making changes. Pain gives people the impulse to fix or change their situation. Sometimes pain is God's way of forcing a congregation to exercise faith and grow stronger:

> Consider it a sheer gift, friends, when tests and challenges come at you from all sides. You know that under pressure, your faith-life is forced into the open and shows its true colors. So don't try to get out of anything prematurely. Let it do its work so you become mature and well-developed, not deficient in any way. (James 1:4-6 TM)

2. Hope

True hope can stimulate change. True hope sees the possibilities of a renewed future and welcomes the new energy and the new ways of doing things that can bring about a new reality. Solomon said, "Hope deferred makes the heart sick, but a longing fulfilled is a tree of life." (Proverbs 13:12 NIV)

3. Vision

When there is a compelling vision and a leadership willing to champion the vision, motivation follows. During a transition, the vision may be short-term, but it can motivate the congregation to make changes, do the necessary work to gain greater health, and prepare for the entrance of the next pastor.

Principle 8: Clarifying Vision Requires Loads of Encouragement.

Encouragement is as necessary to the vision-clarifying process as air is to human beings. People grow discouraged and lose their way when expectations are not met or change becomes bogged down. Encouragement means putting courage into people's hearts and souls so they can press on. Clarifying vision is hard work and is not for the faint of heart. That is why Paul prayed:

> May the God who gives endurance and encouragement give you a spirit of unity among yourselves as you follow Christ Jesus, so that with one heart and mouth you may glorify the God and Father of our Lord Jesus Christ. (Romans 15:5-6 NIV)

> Effective leaders sprinkle encouragement into everything they say and do. Paul told Timothy to integrate encouragement into his ministry: "Preach the Word; be prepared in season and out of season; correct, rebuke and encourage — with great patience and careful instruction." (2 Timothy 4:2 NIV)

Encouraging leaders set a lofty goal before people and treat them as they can become, not as they are. What Stephen R. Covey says about individuals is also true about congregations: "Treat a man as he is and he will remain as he is. Treat a man as he can and should be and he will become as he can and should be."

Principle 9: Outside Coaching Can Increase the Vision-clarifying Impact.

The person who leads the vision-clarifying process is critically important to its success. Sometimes the coach or facilitator comes from within the congregation, but usually it is an outsider. This objectivity serves the congregation well as long as the facilitator has the necessary skills and competencies to do the work. During a pastoral transition, the transitional leader can serve as the facilitator of the vision-clarifying process if that leader has the necessary skills to do so. If the leader does not have those skills, the leader needs to partner with others who have skill and experience in this area.

Here are some of the benefits of having an outside person facilitating the vision-clarifying process:

- An outside coach can hold the congregation's feet to the fire and encourage the members to complete what they started.
- A seasoned coach brings a wealth of experience and can bring examples of how other congregations have navigated the vision-clarifying process.
- Agreeing to a coaching partnership signifies a tangible commitment on the part of the congregation and its leadership to do the hard work required for this process to succeed.
- An outside coach brings access to resources invisible to the congregation.
- An outside coach brings objectivity and helps a congregation see areas needing attention that those

within the congregation no longer see because of their familiarity.

Partnering with a coach is a way to apply the collective wisdom of the body of Christ to the congregation in transition. Paul's admonition to the church in Ephesus speaks to this: "So be careful how you live. Don't live like fools, but like those who are wise. Make the most of every opportunity in these evil days. Don't act thoughtlessly, but understand what the Lord wants you to do." (Ephesians 5:15-17 NIV)

Principle 10: How Far You Get in the Vision-clarifying Process Will Vary.

One question asked during the vision-clarifying process in a transition is: "How much of the vision-clarifying and ministry-planning process should be completed before the next senior pastor arrives?" The answer varies, depending on the type of church, the strength of the leadership, the church governance structure, and other factors.

As a general rule, it usually makes sense to proceed with the first three phases of the vision-clarifying process before the new pastor arrives: assess the situation, build statements and profiles, and clarify the vision.

Going through the process of doing an assessment and building profile statements will help a congregation gain clarity about who it is, why it exists, what it values, and who its community is. Engaging in the vision-clarifying phase helps the congregation think through how God is leading, without the next pastor's influence. The benefit of *not* having the next pastor present is that it may give greater clarity to the question of what kind of pastor the congregation needs for the next season of its ministry.

As far as the action plan is concerned, it makes sense to wait for the next pastor to arrive before developing a detailed plan. A plan is necessary to keep the congregation moving forward during a transition, but this is a short-term plan tied to a vision adopted for the pastoral transition. Since the pastor will be instrumental in carrying out the larger vision, it is wise to have the pastor help develop that plan so as to increase ownership of that plan.

The key to any vision-clarifying process is to realize that both the congregation and the leadership have a stake in seeing the vision become a reality. Some form of congregational involvement in assessment, profile building, and vision clarification will increase involvement when it comes time for action.

Reflective Questions

❖ What are the signs a congregation is ready to engage in vision clarification?

❖ What is the best way in your tradition to hear God speak during a vision-clarifying process?

❖ What tools have you found helpful in vision clarification and ministry planning?

Ministry Planning and the LifePlan Process

LifePlan is a ministry planning resource provided by our denomination. During church transitions, it is recommended that the tool be used because it contributes greatly to the creation of a church profile and the development of the new pastor's job description.

I have used the LifePlan process in a number of transitions I have led. The genius of the LifePlan is that it invites participation from a wide spectrum of the congregation. It also incorporates valuable information from Statistics Canada, from community leaders, and from people within the local congregation. The outcome of the LifePlan is a list of prioritized strategic initiatives which describe a two-year vision for the church.

Here is one example of how it helped a small rural congregation during a transitional time. We put together a small team of people from the congregation and described the LifePlan process to them. Initially there was some resistance, but eventually we gained their willingness to enter the process.

Once the team agreed to proceed, they not only cooperated but engaged fully in gathering information from various sources. The team did a superb job of understanding the information and interpreting the implications for this little village church. We then presented the findings to the congregation in a one-page report, asking the congregation members to prayerfully ask God what this might mean for this church.

The next step was to facilitate a dream session. This little congregation engaged fully. Almost 100 percent of the congregation stayed after church one Sunday to enjoy a potluck meal, followed by the session. I observed as three leaders led the small group discussions around the tables. Conversations were focused, brainstorming guidelines were followed, and ideas were written on sheets of newsprint.

When it came time for each group to report its ideas, I was amazed at the important ideas shared. A creative list of strategic initiatives was developed. Then came the prioritizing component. I watched as a small group of seniors and middle-aged people together discovered how God wanted to lead this church into the future and what kind of leader the church would need for the task.

During the remainder of the transition, we engaged in ministries targeting those strategic initiatives. Today, a leader is in place with clear vision statements before him. Also, lay leaders know this to be a process to be repeated as they continue to move forward with their vision.

— Dennis Camplin

Chapter 10

Facilitating Organizational Health

O rganizational health is a broad category encompassing a number of areas, all having to do with the structure of a congregation's life and ministry. Organizational health is a necessary support and complement to the God-sized vision and ministry plan already discussed. This chapter begins by defining organizational health and then explores some of the main pillars of healthy organization.

> "The single greatest advantage any company (*or church*) can achieve is organizational health. Yet it is ignored by most leaders even though it is simple, free, and available to anyone who wants it."
> — Patrick Lencioni in *The Advantage*

A congregation can become stuck during a pastoral transition when it does not give enough attention to organizational health. If transitional leadership focuses only on the preaching, the Sunday service experience, pastoral care, and ministry activities, to the neglect of overall organizational health, there will be a negative impact, in both the short term and the long term.

Defining Organizational Health

Organizational health is connected closely to the Hebrew and Greek words for *peace*. Peace is "the state of being complete, being whole, or having integrity between all inter-related parts." A congregation is organizationally healthy when its mission and management are aligned and producing the fruit Christ is looking for.

Organizational health is about strengthening the supportive structures of a congregation so the work of the Spirit can thrive. Without a skeleton, the human body falls limp to the ground. Without organization, a congregation falls flat on its face—it may have good intentions, but there is no way to sustain momentum or turn vision into action.

As discussed in Chapter 9, management is one of the aspects held in tension with vision, relationships, and programming. Management is part of organizational health and is tied to the completeness God desires for his church: "For God is not a God of disorder but of peace—as in all the congregations of the Lord's people." (1 Corinthians 14:33 NIV)

Five Pillars of Organization Health

There are a number of crucial areas requiring focused attention when facilitating organizational health. These can be called pillars. In Ephesians, Paul used the metaphor of a house to describe a congregation:

> Together, we are his house, built on the foundation of the apostles and the prophets. And the cornerstone is Christ Jesus himself. We are carefully joined together in him, becoming a holy temple for the Lord. (Ephesians 2:20-21 NLT)

In a building, pillars support the roof and walls and keep them from caving in. Pillars are strategically placed and balanced so they work together. In some buildings, they

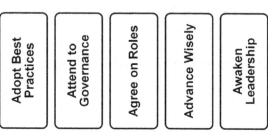

Figure 10: Five Pillars of Organizational Health

are not even visible once the building is up. In a congregation, the pillars are the principles and practices that provide the strength to support the vision and purpose of a congregation.

Pillar 1: Adopt Best Practices

A "best practice" is a procedure or method that has been proven by experience and research to produce a desired result. When a congregation decides to use best practices, it is making a commitment to use all the knowledge and expertise at its disposal to ensure healthy outcomes.

Adopting a best practice isn't easy or automatic. For reasons deeply rooted in history, many congregations tend to resist best practices. They cling to inherited ways of doing things even when they know those ways have failed in the past. A transition provides an opportunity to shift congregational habits towards best practices in the area of organizational health.

Here are nine best practices to consider adopting:

1. Communicate more, not less.

The number one complaint from congregational participants during a pastoral transition is the lack of communication from the leadership. Ineffective communication leads to confusion and discomfort. Chris Gambill of the Center for Congregational Health says, "The primary way to decrease discomfort and anxiety and to increase trust during a transition is through communication: intentional, consistent, multi-modal communication."[30]

People have a genuine need to talk about what is happening or what appears to be happening. Leaders, especially during a transition, are obligated to devote sufficient time to spreading good gossip—in order to prevent the spread of bad gossip. Good gossip builds a sense of community based on shared information and shared values.

When leaders freely share information, they are treating congregational participants as adults, not as infants who need parenting. Aside from the potential legal ramifications of going public with certain information, most information can be entrusted to the congregation, as long as it is communicated properly.

2. Evaluate progress and programs.

Intentional evaluation pushes past the urge to maintain the status quo during a transition and wait until the next pastor arrives to make significant changes. If leaders develop a culture of evaluation during a transition, this mindset can continue after the transition and be built into the culture of the congregation.

Author Ken Blanchard says, "Feedback is the breakfast of champions." That is why leaders should make use of evaluation, performance reviews, and one-on-one coaching sessions. Teams, committees, staff, and other groups should also be taught to practice ongoing and regular evaluation. It is also beneficial to evaluate giving patterns, attendance records, ministry activities, and programs. The information gleaned might shed light on what changes need to be made to achieve greater health and kingdom effectiveness.

3. Ensure authority and responsibility are equal.

The leadership "apple cart" is often upset when a senior pastor leaves. The responsibilities held by the exiting pastor are now up for grabs. This shift can cause confusion about who has the right to make decisions and take responsibility for various areas of ministry. It's essential to clarify matters related to authority and responsibility.

When leaders use authority without taking responsibility for decisions, they tend to be domineering, dictatorial, or even abusive. When leaders have been given responsibility without the authority to make decisions, they feel frustrated and often abused (although few would admit it). When a congregation is organizationally healthy, those with decision-making authority have equal responsibility, and vice versa—in every area of ministry.

4. Make meetings meaningful.

Anyone can hold a meeting, but not every meeting is worth holding. James T. Kirk said, "A meeting is an event where minutes are taken and hours wasted." Meetings do not need to be like that.

To make meetings meaningful, several ingredients are required. These include: a clear purpose; agreed-upon communication guidelines; freedom to participate; skilled facilitation; valid information; a safe and comfortable environment; agreed-upon starting and ending times; follow-through on decisions made during the meeting; trust between participants; productive conflict leading to better decisions; and a climate of love and respect between people.

5. Clarify the decision-making process.

The number one cause of negative conflict within congregations is the way decisions are made. One of the reasons for this is the diversity of people's backgrounds in a congregation now. Fifty years ago, congregations and even denominations were homogeneous. That is no longer the case. There is no consensus on "the way things are done around here" because members no longer come at these questions from a background of shared experience. If, for example, negative conflict arises over the way a congregation chooses a new board member, selects a summer program for children, or determines the amount paid to staff members, the congregation's decision-making process needs to be looked at.

The key to moving forward is to facilitate a conversation (or more than one) around this issue. That conversation can be informed by looking at church policy, denominational distinctives, biblical principles, and best practices. Gaining greater health in the area of decision making during a pastoral transition will reap much fruit once the next pastor arrives and starts to work with the congregation.

6. Develop an emotionally intelligent organization.

Emotional intelligence (known as EQ) is necessary for success in individual and community life. EQ competencies include empathy, intuition, creativity, flexibility, resilience, stress management, leadership, integrity, optimism—and communication skills. By using emotional intelligence in community life, transitional leaders can improve decision making and problem solving.

Marcia Hughes speaks about emotions in the workplace this way:

> Historically, leaders in most organizations have neglected emotions in the workplace. Today we realize that emotions are very much a part of workplace success. How individuals respond to real situations each and every day and what organizations do to foster productive emotional responses can make the difference between the organization that stumbles and the organization that thrives.[31]

An emotionally intelligent congregation maximizes its potential for ministry success and increases fruitfulness.

7. Embrace conflict and peace.

Where two or more are gathered, there will be differences. Conflict, tension over differences, can produce opportunities for healthy growth or destructive abrasion. Like sandpaper, conflict has the potential to smooth off rough spots and rough up smooth spots. The transitional leader should help the congregation determine which spots need roughing up and which need smoothing over.

A healthy organization embraces the spiritual, educational, and healing value of conflict. Conflict is not necessarily bad, even when it feels uncomfortable. The determining factor is the ability or inability to respond to conflict with Christ-like maturity. The key is to be comfortable with being uncomfortable.

When conflict arises in a congregation, the transitional leader should work at making genuine peace. This is accomplished not by being a peacekeeper (holding two warring factions apart) but by being a peacemaker (bringing the sides together to work towards reconciliation). Peacemaking is consistent with Paul's words: "Let us therefore make every effort to do what leads to peace and to mutual edification." (Romans 14:19 NIV)

8. Use Appreciative Inquiry to find life in the congregation.

Every congregation has a life of its own. This life is enhanced or hindered by the activities of its members. Therefore, it is prudent to determine what brings life to the congregation and what detracts from the abundant life God has in mind. One way to approach this discovery is through Appreciative Inquiry (AI).[32] AI is a collaborative and participatory approach that identifies and builds on the life-giving forces within an organization.

Identifying, highlighting, and encouraging what is currently working will boost the health of a congregation. AI helps keep a congregation focused on hope in the midst of change. It helps produce the momentum required for transitioning from the past to the future. This approach can work well in partnership with a vision-clarifying process.

9. Balance the organic and the organized nature of a congregation.

Another aspect of congregational life concerns the dynamic tension between the organized and the organic nature of the church. Both aspects are essential for organizational health.

When a congregation is overly organized, it limits organic life—it resembles a skeleton without flesh. Much is accomplished through organization, but if it is without the life and power of the Spirit, it amounts to wasted effort. Ezekiel gives us hope by describing how God can breathe life into dry bones and bring the dead back to life (Ezekiel 37). It requires prayer and a humble dependence on God to shift the focus of a congregation from too much organization.

The opposite extreme to dry bones is chaos, an abundance of energy without adequate structure. It's like having a rushing river without river banks—which results in a destructive flood. If a congregation focuses on the emotional and interpersonal aspects of its life, to the detriment of structure and organization, it will be weak and vulnerable. The lack of structure will lead to an inward focus, self-love, and a narcissistic approach to ministry. Change requires humility and the willingness to put in place the checks and balances necessary to support ongoing ministry.

Organizational Wisdom

It is strategically important to recognize that local churches are both organisms and organizations. As an organism, the local church is a body similar to the human body. It has visible and invisible parts which are bound together by muscles and ligaments and which are controlled by the head. The local church, like a human body, lives and breathes. It has life. In this manner, it is different and more wonderful than any other organization in the world.

The local church is one of the most amazing creations of God in the entire universe, designed to be totally different from any other collection of individuals related to each other. It is a body that feeds on the Word of God and is controlled by the Holy Spirit; it thinks, moves, works, and feels. It is marked by the love and consideration of each part of the body for every other part. A healthy church, like a healthy body, responds immediately and obediently to the dictates and desires of the head; if it doesn't, it is spastic and disabled.

The local church, however, is also an organization not all that different in structure from other organizations.

It is composed of members and appointed leaders. It exists not only for fellowship, but for functional reasons as well.

It usually has a defined reason for its existence, commonly called a mission statement. It often has a vision, where it looks into the future to see how it can fulfill the goals God has marked out.

A local church is a legal entity; it is incorporated like other organizations or societies. It is subject to the laws of the land. It is governed by bylaws and policies, and is usually led by a small group of its members, in whom the congregation has confidence and trust. We call them the "board."

Local churches are not the only organizations with boards, members, and a specified relationship between them. If the local church is to accomplish something specific, it must go through the steps of planning, organization, and control (meaning that it must ensure the outcome adheres to the plan).

All management, leadership, and administration are based on planning, organization, and accountability. A local church must go through these steps if it hopes to enjoy harmonious relationships and success in its work. If it is to accomplish anything, it must have competent leadership and a committed following.

Leaders must practice sound principles of delegation, accountability, and responsibility. The heart of leadership, management, and administration is delegation. The pastoral office has a management function as well as a shepherding role.

Jesus Christ was and is the greatest management figure the world has ever seen. The life and ministry of Jesus followed the same principles the gurus of management advocate today. God is the ultimate manager. The key to happy, harmonious relationships and productive, fulfilling ministry is the application of biblical management principles with agape love. This will set us miles ahead of any secular organization.

— Doug Harris

Pillar 2: Attend to Governance

One place where ill health in an organization is easily noticed is in the area of church governance. It is not uncommon for congregational leaders to be unfamiliar with the written documents describing their governance structure. This leads to confusion and unnecessary conflict as they rely on their previous experiences and understanding to interpret current board practice.

A pastoral transition creates an opportunity to review, renew, and commit to a governance structure and organizational model that has broad support. A basic understanding of the three major models (Episcopal, Presbyterian, and Congregational) will help the transitional leader determine how to approach and work within each model. Which model is correct based on New Testament teaching? We believe no one model is the perfect model. On the contrary, various models have emerged throughout history for different reasons, based on various theological foundations.

Model 1: Episcopal

The Episcopal model, also called the hierarchical model, is seen in Roman Catholic, Anglican, and charismatic churches. The word "episcopal" comes from the Greek word *episcopos*, which means "overseer" or "superintendent."

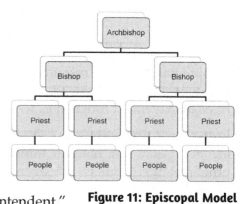

Figure 11: Episcopal Model

Episcopos was used in Koine Greek to designate a government official and is translated in the King James Version of the Bible as "bishop." The Episcopal model refers to a system of church government which is hierarchical. The church is ruled by overseers, usually called "bishops" or "leaders."

Model 2: Presbyterian

In the Presbyterian model, a congregation is governed by a group of presbyters, elders, or priests. This system originated in the Old Testament synagogue, where authority over the congregation was vested in the elders.

In some Presbyterian systems, the elders are appointed by the congregation. In others, they are recommended by the Presbytery (or group of elders) and ratified by the congregation. In still others, they are appointed by the board of elders with minimal congregational involvement, which turns the eldership (sometimes called "oversight") into a self-perpetuating board. In some Presbyterian and Brethren systems, the elders are divided into "ruling elders" and "teaching elders." In this system, the designation "pastor" is given to a teaching elder.

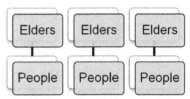

Figure 12: Presbyterian Model

Model 3: Congregational

In the Congregational model, the congregation may delegate leadership responsibilities but final authority rests with the people, and the leaders are ultimately accountable to the congregation. Congregational church government means the church is ruled by the gathered congregation. The key issue in the Congregational model is to determine where the authority lies to make decisions on behalf of the congregation. If the congregation and its leaders hold to the Congregational model, boards and pastors must be willing to submit to congregational authority.

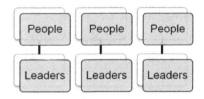

Figure 13: Congregational Model

Cautionary Notes for Transitional Leaders

Transitional leaders must demonstrate sensitivity to the congregation's governance model and culture. It is crucial to determine clear authority lines for the pastor, the board, committees, and other

> "You can only hold people accountable to what they agree to."
> — TJ Addington

leaders. These lines of authority need to be described in writing and be consistent with the constitution and bylaws. When lines of authority are clear, conflict and misunderstanding will be reduced, especially during times of stress.

It's important to recognize that there may be a difference between the transitional leader's preferred governance model and the chosen model of the congregation. Sometimes a transitional leader has an urge to change the governance model of a congregation. The rule of thumb when considering this intervention is this: the transitional leader should only change or modify a congregation's governance when clearly mandated to do so.

A better question to answer regarding governance is this: "What does this congregation require to make its governance model healthy and effective (without changing it to fit the transitional leader's preferred style)?"

Here are a few other issues for the transitional leader to consider when assessing the health of a congregation's governance:

- The transitional leader should work to increase awareness of and compliance with the agreed-upon governance model.
- The leader should be aware of any gap between the written and practiced governance models.
- The leader should be aware that multiple governance models may exist in the minds of the people in the congregation.
- The leader should ask insightful questions about how things work and how decisions are made.

- The leader should recognize and honor the congregation's denominational history, affiliation, and tradition.
- The leader should resist the urge to jump to conclusions based on his or her personal assumptions.
- The leader should be curious and make observations about common decision-making practices.
- The leader should remember that he or she is not there to judge the congregation's chosen governance model but to guide the congregation towards health (unless this has specifically been made part of the transitional leader's mandate).
- The transitional leader should know his or her authority and responsibility within the transitional agreement for changing or renewing the governance model.
- The leader should follow the principle "Give to those who ask" unless harm is being done to the congregation as a result of poor management

Pillar 3: Agree on Roles and Responsibilities

Clearly defined and agreed-upon roles and responsibilities for leaders within a congregation are vital to organizational health. When roles and responsibilities are clear, everyone benefits. The benefits will be felt during the transition and will continue to be felt when the next pastor arrives. The transitional leader should facilitate the necessary conversations with three key groups to make this a reality:

1. Positional and Functional Leaders

It's helpful to understand the roles of both positional leaders and functional leaders (official and unofficial leaders). The typical congregation will have people in official positions but not necessarily functioning well in those positions. These persons may be filling vacancies with willing hearts but may not have what is needed to do the work well. On the flip side, there may be people who have no official positions but who have a high level of giftedness and ministry effectiveness.

It is a joy when the right people are in the right positions, doing the right things for the right reasons. When the transitional leader understands these dynamics, values each individual's contribution, and works with all groups, it will benefit the congregation's overall organizational health.

2. Key Influencers

Identifying the key influencers (also called powerbrokers) will assist the transitional leader in clarifying and managing roles and responsibilities within a congregation. There are influencers who operate for the good of the congregation and those who are self-motivated towards personal gain and control. Wherever people organize, there will be politics at work. Politics can be defined as "maneuvering within a group of people in order to gain control or power."

A word of caution: Negatively labeling people often reinforces negative outcomes. People may change roles depending on how others perceive them. A negative powerbroker may become a positive influencer for the good of the whole congregation if that person is made to feel trusted and is allowed to have a voice.

3. Dissenting Voices

During a pastoral transition, previously defined roles can become blurred. This creates an opportunity for the politically motivated to assert their views or become aggressive in their maneuvering for power. They may behave this way while at the same time believing they are doing God's work. Some will see the senior pastor vacuum as an opportunity to influence people towards their own agenda, unrealized under the exiting pastor. The transitional leader will need the gift of discernment to properly read the situation and decide if church discipline or correction is required.

A word of caution: Not all dissenting voices are motivated by willful resistance. Sometimes people may be simply expressing their thoughts or feelings but not have the skill to do so calmly.

Dissenting voices have a role in bringing issues to the forefront, so leaders should listen carefully and discern what God might be saying through these voices. After hearing these voices, it's important for the leaders to decide prayerfully and carefully how to respond. Leaders are responsible for providing channels of communication through which members of the congregation can raise their concerns and speak from their hearts without being stepped on.

Pillar 4: Advance Wisely

The timing for doing organizational renewal is very important for a successful outcome. Four factors impact when the time is right to step into the work of facilitating organizational health:

1. Consider the circumstances of the previous pastor's exit.

Depending on the context of the previous pastor's exit, adjustments to organizational health may be relatively easy. If the pastor's exit was smooth, organizational renewal can be considered early on in the transition. If the pastor's exit was a rough or crisis exit, work in the areas of closure and relationship renewal will be needed before organizational renewal can be attempted. Ongoing assessment and spiritual discernment will help the transitional leadership determine the congregation's readiness for taking the next steps.

2. Consider the change readiness of the congregation.

Change readiness impacts organizational renewal. If a congregation knows it needs to change and is ready to change, the transitional leadership can get on with it. If the answer to the question, "Do you want to get well?" is "Yes, but..." or "We think we're fine," the soil for change still needs cultivation.

Sometimes readiness for organizational renewal occurs when the current organization has caused sufficient pain to convince people that it isn't working. In other situations, readiness follows a clear vision or sufficient awareness of why "there" is better than "here."

3. Consider the level of trust given to the transitional leader.

If the transitional leader is to be the point person for leading organizational renewal, the leader must first earn the congregation's trust. Temporary trust is often given to the transitional leader, but that trust must be tested before it is solidified. When trust has been tested and confirmed, people will follow the leader because they want to, not just because of the leader's position. Trust is earned through consistency, patience, and integrity.

> "Trust is the conviction that the leader means what he or she says. It is a belief in two old-fashioned qualities called consistency and integrity. Trust opens the door to change."
> — Peter Drucker

Once genuine trust has been earned, the transitional leader can lead the congregation into organizational renewal with confidence. If the level of trust remains low, the transitional leader will be able to provide pastoral services, but will not be able to facilitate deep change.

4. Consider the three phases of organization renewal: stability, cohesion, and momentum.

Organizational renewal moves through three phases. It begins with stabilizing the congregation's emotions and ministry, moves on to developing cohesion in community life, and finally ends with building momentum for organizational renewal.

Each phase requires attention before moving on to the next. The stabilization phase includes the reduction of tears and fears, the subsiding of negative talk about the pastor's exit, and the development of a sense that things are going to be OK. Cohesion shows up in the form of longer conversations between people, spontaneous gatherings, and motivation for collective projects. Momentum for organizational renewal results when the previous two phases are well established.

Pillar 5: Awaken the Leadership Gift

Leadership is the immune system of the body. Maintaining and improving the spiritual, emotional, and relational strength of the leadership community strengthens organizational health. The first line of defense against threats and negative influences attacking a congregation is a healthy leadership community. Four factors improve the strength of the leadership:

> "Healthy congregations develop an immune system. They do not let pathogens inflict harm on the community. Mature leadership gives the congregation wise blood."
> — Peter L. Steinke

1. Spiritual and Personal Development

Someone once said, "God's gift to us: potential. Our gift to God: developing it." This is true of individual Christians and of Christian organizations. For a congregation to be healthy organizationally, its leaders need to be continually growing and developing, both individually and as a community.

This means that leaders should be growing spiritually, emotionally, mentally, and relationally. This includes practicing the spiritual disciplines (prayer, meditation, Scripture reading, fasting, confession) and living as an example to the congregation. It means the leaders should be growing in emotional intelligence and working out any differences they may have with one another. The glue that holds a leadership community together is love: "A new command I give you: Love one another. As I have loved you, so you must love one another." (John 13:34 NIV)

2. Shared Purpose and Values

A lack of shared purpose and values can be fatal for a leadership community. Conversely, having a shared purpose and shared values breathes life into a community. Paul's admonition to the church in Philippi reinforces this truth: "Then make me truly happy by agreeing wholeheartedly with each other, loving one another, and working together with one mind and purpose." (Philippians 2:2 NLT)

When the leadership community is unified, discouragement and distraction will be held at bay. When leaders spend time reviewing and recommitting themselves to a biblical purpose and a common set of core values, it strengthens the congregation's immune system and keeps life flowing in the congregational veins.

3. Open and Transparent Communication

Nothing destroys trust and increases negative and unnecessary conflict like bad communication. James gives us a three-part lesson on how to communicate:

> Post this at all the intersections, dear friends: Lead with your ears, follow up with your tongue, and let anger straggle along in the rear. God's righteousness doesn't grow from human anger. So throw all spoiled virtue and cancerous evil in the garbage. In simple humility, let our gardener, God, landscape you with the Word, making a salvation-garden of your life. (James 1:19-21 TM)

Effective communication happens when leaders listen carefully, speak from a place of understanding, and manage their emotions so that they respond with respect and love. As God acts as the gardener and does his "landscape work" in the leaders, the leaders will be able to communicate from a biblically informed perspective.

4. Congregational Awareness and Trust

As Peter F. Drucker wisely said, "Organizations are built on trust, and trust is built on communication and mutual understanding." It is not only the trust between leaders that is important, but also the trust between the leadership community and the congregation.

It is not uncommon in medium to large congregations to hear that certain members of the congregation don't know who is on the church board or what the church board members do. The time between pastors can be an opportunity to increase the visibility of congregational leaders and build trust between the congregation and its leaders.

> "A beautiful thing happens when we start paying attention to each other. It is by participating more in your relationship that you breathe life into it."
> — Steve Maraboli

Awareness of and trust in congregational leaders can be built in a number of ways: by the congregation hearing the leaders declare their intentions; by the congregation seeing leaders involved and participating in public services and ministries; and by leaders learning to find other ways to connect with congregational members in meaningful and positive ways.

Reflective Questions

❖ What is the relationship between organizational health, relationship renewal, and vision clarity?

❖ What is the danger in a transitional leader imposing a particular style of governance on a congregation without permission or proper assessment?

❖ How do you determine whether organizational change should occur before the next pastor arrives or after the next pastor arrives?

A Story of Governance Renewal

The transitional leader presented a "mind map" of the board's current governance model on the wall. It detailed the leadership structure, the decision-making process, and the policies for managing staff, programs, and finances. It was well laid out and had been fully explained in written documents found in the congregational archives.

The room was silent. One board member asked, "What church does this represent?" Another pointed to the title and said, "It's our church, but I haven't seen this document in years." It was glaringly apparent to the transitional leader that this current board and several previous boards were not familiar with the written document containing the policies and procedures they were supposed to be operating by.

As the meeting progressed, it became clear there was a significant gap between the written policy documents and the current practice. Three critical decisions were made that day: 1) every board member (both staff members and congregational leaders) would read the documents; 2) the board would renew its commitment to adhere to these documents without unnecessarily disturbing the status quo; and 3) the board would put together an organizational renewal team to review and recommend changes to close the gap between the written and practiced governance models.

— Alan Simpson

God Works to Bring Organizational Health

While I was providing transitional leadership in a church in a progressive Canadian prairie town, it became apparent to me that change was needed. This church had experienced significant growth during the ministry of a long-term pastor but now needed to process a number of issues to become healthy enough to move into a new future.

When I arrived, the church board consisted of at least 14 people and was structured as a "representative" board. This meant that ministry leaders and chairpeople of various church committees and departments became the board of the church. At the time of this transition, there was evidence of tension and division among the members of the board. The board functioned basically as a management board.

One of my early recommendations was for the board to be restructured to function as a governance board and for the ministry leaders to form a ministry team to help the church move in the direction of its vision. We studied different styles of board structure and recommended to the membership a new direction to take, which the members approved. Over the next several weeks, the process of nominating suitable candidates who matched the posted profile for the governance board was followed.

The process produced 14 candidates for seven positions on the board. From the wide variety of nominees who were willing to serve if elected, it was evident that there was tension within the congregation. At the general meeting where the election of the new board would take place, there was a significant turnout of members. Though they were polite to one another, the seating arrangements and the hum of chatter in the pre-meeting period indicated tensions were just below the surface. At the same time, people saw progress being made and felt both apprehension and anticipation.

Reports were heard. Routine agenda items were processed. Finally, it came time to elect the new board. A ballot with the names of the 14 candidates was distributed, and the members were given time to indicate the seven of their choice. The rule was that each board member needed to be elected with a majority vote. I was anticipating a long night, with the tedious task of working our way through several ballots in order to select the seven.

The ballots were collected and sent with the tellers for tabulation. The meeting continued with other business items. We waited. No report from the tellers. We took a break. Still the tellers had no report. Then, finally, when the report came back, the chairman reported the names of the seven persons who had been elected, with a majority vote, on the first ballot!

We all knew this was a "God moment." The previous underlying tension quickly changed to a settledness, calmness, and affirmation of how God was indeed leading us in the direction of our future—a future including restored unity and creation of a common vision.

— Dennis Camplin

Chapter 11

Facilitating the Search Process

T he optimum time for a congregation to begin an active search for the next senior pastor is after sufficient health and unity has been achieved. Since "sufficient health" is a matter of opinion and subjective in nature, it's wise to agree at the beginning of the transition what transitional goals need to be reached before a search will begin.

It's critical for a congregation to lay aside anxiety when it comes to finding the next pastor. If anxiety is the prevailing emotional reality, the search process will be flawed and inconsistent with God's pathway for doing his work from a place of peace and faith:

> Don't worry about anything; instead, pray about everything. Tell God what you need, and thank him for all he has done. Then you will experience God's peace, which exceeds anything we can understand. His peace will guard your hearts and minds as you live in Christ Jesus. (Philippians 4:6-7 NLT)

This chapter will explore six critical issues and four phases of the search process. While the search process goes on, it's essential to remain open to the unique work of God in the congregation and in the heart and life of the person who will become the next pastor.

One Search Team's Story

The congregation of 50 was located on a small island on the west coast of Canada. This was the congregation's first official pastoral search in the 18 years of its history.

The search team had compiled the responses from its comprehensive advertising and networking efforts over the past several weeks. A total of 94 resumes had been sent in from South Africa, Kenya, the US, the UK, India, Nepal, and Canada. The team considered a short list of 44 candidates.

The congregation had hired a transitional leader to assist with preaching and pastoral care but did not think initially it would need him to help with the search. As the search process progressed, the transitional leader asked to attend one of the search team's meetings to offer support and to pray for the team.

In the meeting, the team was evaluating several candidates. One serious candidate had a favorite doctrine, on which he had written a book. The phone call interview with him had gone well, and one search team member commented, "He sounds like a really nice guy." The transitional leader cautiously offered a question about his doctrine: "How will his favorite doctrine influence your congregational culture and view of the church?" Silence and then confusion entered the room.

It was obvious to the transitional leader that the preferred doctrine of the candidate was miles apart from the doctrine of the congregation. The question prompted a healthy conversation and resulted in a request for more input from the transitional leader on the process of selecting a candidate. The transitional leader assisted the search team with thoughtful questions and careful observations without trying to influence the search team's selection. The team was able to reduce the list to three top candidates and select one who was a great fit for the congregation.

— Alan Simpson

Six Critical Issues in Facilitating the Search Process

1. Understand Organizational Culture

It is critical for the transitional leader to understand the governance culture of the congregation as it searches for a new pastor. Key questions include: Who ultimately hires the new pastor? Is there a bylaw or constitutional document informing this question? Is there congruence between the documents and the congregation's practice? Where does the authority lie? To find the right answer, the transitional leader might want to talk to the board, the personnel committee, or the congregation as a whole.

Another consideration is for the transitional leader to be aware of the guidelines used in the search process. How will the final decision be made? Will it be by a congregational vote based on Robert's Rules of Order, through listening prayer, or by following *Roberta's Rules* (a real book title)? Whatever organizational system is in place, the transitional leader, board, search team, and congregation need to be aware of the guidelines and agree ahead of time on the process that will be followed.

2. Involve the Congregation in the Process

In some congregations, the leadership hires a new pastor without informing the congregation until the decision is made. In other settings, the congregation is fully engaged in determining what kind of pastor matches its situation and who will ultimately be hired. It is important to agree ahead of time on how much the congregation will be involved in the search process.

Congregational involvement might include a congregational survey and a follow-up process to prepare both a church profile and a pastor profile. Prayer involvement might be another way to keep the congregation engaged; a flow of accurate information to the congregation will be necessary to keep the prayers relevant. In addition, spiritually mature individuals will be an asset for understanding the congregation and discerning its needs.

3. Study the Search Process History

Unless the congregation is a church plant, it will have a history of hiring pastors. The history of success and failure in previous searches will help those involved now to walk in the strengths and avoid the pitfalls of the past. History often repeats itself unless the congregation's leaders learn from it and intentionally make adjustments. Interviewing previous search team members will inform the transitional leader and current search team about how to proceed with greater health and success.

Another historical question to ask is: What was the hiring experience of the previous pastors? If possible, it would be helpful to interview previous or current pastors about the process when they were hired. What worked? Where did the search process get stuck? What steps were missed? This information will strengthen the search team by helping it avoid mistakes and stay on track.

4. Practice Sensitivity to the Spirit of God

The process of searching for a pastor is different from other employee recruitment processes. The process that a search team and congregation engage in should be based on spiritual discernment. Unfortunately, prayer and dependence on God are sometimes underutilized or halfheartedly pursued. This does not need to be the norm. Earnest and consistent prayer, asking the Father to direct the search process, is of paramount importance.

A congregation often receives the kind of pastor it has the faith to believe for and the persistent prayer to ask for. Hand-in-hand with persistent prayer is the need for surrender. As people surrender to God, it allows him to break into hearts and change minds about what the congregation thinks it needs. Lingering with God in prayer adjusts viewpoints and results in an alignment with his will.

Another spiritual aspect of this process involves the heart and head preparation of the congregation. God wants to do a deep work in the members of a congregation before giving them a new leader. A congregation which rushes the process might not be ready to receive the next pastor. Unresolved issues, negative patterns, and unhealthy dependence on one person might be some of the problems God wants to fix by his Spirit in the midst of the chaos of transition. God is a master at creating order out of chaos. Creation is a testimony to that fact.

5. Begin the Search at the Appropriate Time

The urge to begin the search process because there is a "leadership void" is sometimes an uncontrollable urge in today's church. If a congregation succumbs to the "urge to search" before the time is right, the opportunity for deep assessment and life-giving adjustment during the transition will be lost. The timing for starting the search is a crucial conversation the leadership needs to have when mapping out the transition process. Creating a strategy and being clear on why the leadership is waiting will help the congregation stay focused and sufficiently patient.

The right time to start the search will emerge as transitional goals are achieved and there develops a readiness in the hearts of the spiritually and emotionally mature. There will be a growing sense that the congregation has invested enough time in the hard work of reflection, repair, and renewal. Waiting too long before starting the search can be hazardous to congregational health as well. Discernment and sensitivity are essential skills to utilize during this time.

6. Maintain Healthy Relationships between Key Players

The sixth critical issue concerns how responsibility and authority are shared among the transitional leader, the board, and the transition team. Each of the key players needs to be clear on roles, expectations, authority, responsibility, lines of communication, and the decision-making process. The transitional leader can assist all key players from tripping over each other or, worse, stepping on each other.

Some key questions to ask when facilitating the search process are:

- What authority does each party have in the search process?
- What responsibility does each party have in the search process?
- To whom are the parties accountable?
- What are the expectations around feedback, communication, timing, the number of candidates, the process for evaluating candidates, and the process for inviting candidates?

Doug Harris shares his wisdom on the search process: "God has a person for every situation who can fulfill his plan and bring joy and blessing to a church. Believing this transforms the pastoral search process into a spiritual one, where hearts are opened wide to hear from him. The search process should be one that opens everyone's senses to where God is already leading the church and where he is working in the heart and life of the one to become the next pastor of the church."[33]

Questions to Clarify the Role of the Transitional Leader

The transitional leader will be called upon to wear a variety of hats during the search process. What's required depends on the skill and experience of the congregation and its leaders. Here are a few questions a transitional leader can ask to determine what role he or she will be filling during the search process:

- **Facilitator** — am I guiding the process without making the decisions?
- **Manager** — am I in charge of the process and making decisions about the process but not decisions about the candidates?
- **Leader** — am I leading the process, with full responsibility for the outcome?

- **Helper** — am I an extra set of hands, coming alongside someone else who is in charge of the process?
- **Coach** — am I supporting the search team by asking questions, listening intently, and providing feedback when appropriate?
- **Consultant** — am I the expert who designs the process and offers expertise to the search team?
- **Entrepreneur** — am I the person with fresh ideas who will invite other leaders to apply for the position?

Four Stages in Facilitating the Search Process

There are four stages to the search process. Being aware of these stages gives a road map to follow and a way to monitor progress throughout the search. The four stages are: preparation, documentation, exploration, and engagement. When the stages are completed in order, in a timely fashion, and with a congregation ready for the search, the process ends with the pastor God has in mind for the congregation.

Stage 1: Preparation

A congregation is encouraged to begin its search with a season of *concentrated prayer*. In order to pray effectively, the congregation needs to receive information. This will enable the members of the congregation to celebrate wins and continue in prayer until an answer comes. Areas where prayer is needed might include the spiritual health of the congregation, unity and focus in decision making, God's preparation of the new pastor, and spiritual eyes to recognize God's choice for this congregation. It's important to practice creativity and think through how prayer can be fostered in each unique congregational context.

Another aspect of preparation is *selecting and training* the people who will do the search. Whether it's the transition team which conducts the search, a separate search team, or the board, it's important to identify the character qualities needed in search team members. The search team should have the same qualities as the transition team (see Chapter 21). As the search team members learn to work together as a team, the possibility of success will go up significantly.

Another aspect of preparation is helping the congregation identify its *values, purpose, and vision* so the congregation can find a suitable pastor to lead in that direction. Arriving at an understanding of the values, purpose, and vision is an interactive process involving surveying the members of the congregation, facilitating conversations, gathering data, reflecting on history, and spending time in prayer.

Stage 2: Documentation

Once the congregation has prepared itself through prayer, selected a search team, and clarified its identity and purpose, it can begin creating a summary report or set of documents for potential candidates. This report can be anything from a glossy portfolio to an online slide show to a printed document. The format of the report is not as important as the message the report communicates. The documents should give a clear picture of the congregation and its ministry, and minimize the possibility of surprises when the new pastor arrives and begins work. Here are a few things to include:

- A description of the congregation's core values, purpose, and vision for the future

This information shows prospective candidates the heart and soul of the congregation. The more closely the written report reflects the actual reality, the better. This description will either have been in place when the congregation went into transition or will have been updated during the transition when the congregation was clarifying its vision. This is one of the reasons it is important to not begin a pastoral search until the basic elements of healthy congregational life are in place.

- A description of the people and ministries of the congregation

This description (sometimes called the "church profile") includes: attendance patterns, giving records, the age breakdown, household income, education, facilities information, program information, organizational structure, leadership structure, staff details, and historical information.

- A description of the community surrounding the congregation

This description (sometimes called the "community profile") gives a snapshot of the surrounding area and the people living there. It includes demographic information (population, income, ethnicity, language, occupations, education, and housing) along with other relevant data.

- A job description for the new senior pastor

A typical job description includes: major responsibilities, key activities, standards of performance, and core competencies (or whatever terms and categories fit the congregation's culture and context). This position description needs to match the culture and future direction of the congregation.

Allowing the congregation access to these documents can be a positive move. If members of the congregation are wanting to recommend candidates, knowing where the congregation is wanting to go will help them see more clearly whether the proposed candidate will fit.

Before beginning an active search, the search team will need to answer a few more questions: What will happen if there are not enough suitable applications? How will we evaluate each applicant? Will the team need to unanimously recommend candidates? What guidelines will we follow as a team to keep us on track? What criteria will we use to know if this person is God's choice?

129

Stage 3: Exploration

This is where the rubber hits the road. The exploration stage is where the search team begins contacting candidates and opening the door for dialogue. The work completed prior to this stage has laid the foundation on which the search team will now build. The exploration stage includes initiating the search, researching and interviewing candidates, tracking and reporting the results, and making a final decision.

In order for candidates to apply for the position, the word must be spread that the position exists. The job description prepared earlier outlines the competencies, skills, and qualities of the type of leader the congregation is looking for. It should be written in a format that can be easily understood and should be attractive to the type of people the search team hopes will apply.

There are many ways to communicate information about a vacant ministry position. The options include ministry job search websites, denominational communication channels, word of mouth, seminary message boards, and conversations with well-connected leaders. The search team might also approach potential candidates it feels are suited to the ministry position. If this approach is used, it is important to follow accepted protocol so confidentiality and boundaries are respected.

Once there are candidates who have shown interest in the position, the search team will begin the process of screening the candidates. The result of the screening process should be to develop a short list of candidates the search team wants to examine further. This process requires teamwork, prayer, and people skills as the search team makes decisions and communicates with both those who are on the short list and those who are not.

The initial interviews with the short-listed candidates—whether by phone, by email, or face to face—are an opportunity to listen, ask questions, and start to become better acquainted. The search team is checking out the candidate, and the candidate is checking out the congregation. The interviews should cover hopes, dreams, leadership style, core beliefs, needs, and experience.

As candidates make their way through the interview process, the search team should be conducting background and reference checks from a place of neutrality and non-judgment. This should be done with the cooperation and support of the candidate. For candidates under serious consideration, the search team may want to visit the candidate's previous (or current) congregation and appropriately speak with people from that congregation. Not gathering enough information on the past ministry of a candidate can prove disastrous.

A word of wisdom on having a potential candidate come and preach: Delay a preaching opportunity until after sufficient screening has been done. One good sermon could persuade the congregation of a candidate's suitability, which could create an awkward situation if further research reveals glaring reasons why the candidate is not a suitable match. It is wise to rely on solid interviewing practices and focused listening prayer more than on subjective feelings.

It is important to document the details of the information collected about each candidate all along. This will keep people and information from falling through the cracks and ensure that the search process has been thorough.

Stage 4: Engagement

Engagement is the process through which the congregation and the candidate reach an agreement for the pastor to begin ministry in the congregation. "Engagement" is not used here in the sense of courtship or dating—which would imply that the process will lead to a marriage that will eventually end in divorce when the pastor exits. "Engagement" is used here in the sense of "to hire for work or assistance" rather than "to give to in marriage."[34]

A mutual agreement between the congregation and the new pastor creates the basis for a healthy working relationship. As the parties work through the details of this agreement, issues such as salary, terms of employment, lines of authority and responsibility, benefits, housing, and special considerations (senior's housing, daycare, building programs in progress, etc.) will need to be discussed.

The transitional leader can assist the search team by facilitating conversations and documenting the terms of the pastor-congregation agreement. A mutual agreement, approved by the congregation, the congregational leadership, and the denomination (if applicable), creates a solid place to begin ministry together.

Where possible, it can be helpful for there to be a conversation between the transitional leader and the incoming pastor. It can also be helpful for there to be a conversation between the previous pastor and the incoming pastor. However. discernment and wisdom should be used when setting up such meetings.

Five Common Errors in the Search Process

1. Not looking at enough candidates

There is no perfect number of candidates to consider, but looking at too few can hinder the search. A suggested selection ratio is four-to-one or five-to-one. That is, for every position, there should be four or five candidates to choose from. Looking at more than one or two candidates forces the search team to do its homework and be careful and prayerful with the search. The search team needs to look at enough candidates that it will be able to find the right person.

2. An inadequate position description

Some pastors do not understand what is expected of them because the position description they were given at the beginning of the process was too vague. In their eagerness and enthusiasm, these pastors may launch out on a course following their own expectations—only to discover six months later the real expectations of the congregation and its leaders.

When the pastor's expectations collide with the mismatched expectations of the congregation, the result can be tension, frustration, and anger. If those differences are not resolved quickly, the result may be the premature exit of the pastor.

3. Incomplete exploration of a candidate's cultural fit

When a candidate is short-listed, a complete exploration of the candidate's background, values, and beliefs needs to done. The culture (values, thinking, beliefs) of the candidate needs to match the culture of the congregation. A poor fit can lead to conflict and the early exit of the pastor.

It is the responsibility of both the candidate and the congregation to know both cultures and make sure they fit with each other. Aubrey Malphurs echoes this point in his book *Look Before You Lead* by saying the candidating pastor "needs to know his culture—the culture he brings with him to the church—and...what he's getting himself into."[35]

4. Ineffective interviewing techniques

One candidate said this about his interview experience: "I had to suggest questions for them to ask me as a candidate." Interviewing is the most widely used method of making selection decisions, but when it is done improperly, it becomes an unreliable predictor of later performance.

If the search team does not understand the issues, it may ask inadequate questions, display inappropriate attitudes, and use ineffective procedures. There is plenty of help available to give a search team the training necessary to be able to interview well.

5. Lack of clear criteria for selection

Often a search team has no criteria on which to base its questions. This will result in the team making decisions based on feelings or presumptions which may or may not be valid. Even if a pastor profile has been developed, the search team might not know how to use it to frame questions for the interview process. A worthwhile conversation to have before starting the search process is to ask questions such as: How will we choose our candidate? What will the stages of the interview process look like?

Reflective Questions

❖ What impact will your past search experience have on any future search team involvement?

❖ What is the role of the transitional leader in the search process and why?

❖ What tools would you add to your list of resources to help make the search process effective and successful?

The Search Team Goes Back to the Drawing Board

I was invited to join a transition team for a congregation which had gone through a very bitter separation from the former pastor. The team consisted of another retired pastor, an administrator, and myself. We were a positive team that had grown close and seen our love for each other grow in significant ways.

The fallout from the previous administration had split the church and reduced it to half its former size. Hurts, anger, and bitterness were everywhere. During my first year of working with the congregation, people settled down and began to rebuild confidence in leadership. We heard comments such as, "It's so good to see leaders working together in harmony."

During that year of transitional ministry, the three of us shared the preaching responsibilities, with some help from a few gifted men in the congregation. From the platform, we freely joked with each other; as we did so, we felt the tension in the congregation melt away. After a year of transition, the congregation was ready to look for another lead pastor.

As the search team was formed, suggestions for the type of leader needed were voiced. The dominant theme was that the new pastor had to be relational but not necessarily a strong preacher since the church had several good teachers. I encouraged the congregation to consider a pastor who was competent in preaching because even though he would share the preaching, I believed the congregation would want a pastor who was solid in his preaching.

The search team was not convinced that I understood the congregation's need and continued its search for a predominantly loving, relational pastor. The man the search team finally recommended to the congregation fit that description very well.

The candidate met with a number of leaders, and they all agreed he was the man they had been looking for. They introduced him to the congregation one Sunday and asked him to preach. The result was a disaster.

The congregation, including the leaders who had endorsed him, were very disappointed in his presentation and rejected him as a candidate. The search team had to go back to the drawing board.

The lesson learned in this situation was this: when building a job description for a lead pastor, keep the long-term needs in mind and don't make a decision based on a feeling or on immediate needs.

— Dennis Scott

Section 3: The Transitional Congregation

"Out of clutter, find simplicity. From discord, find harmony. In the middle of difficulty lies opportunity."

— Albert Einstein

I f you are a congregation in the midst of a pastoral transition, or if you are working with a congregation about to experience a pastoral transition in the near future, this section is for you. Although a pastoral transition can be a time of uncertainty and emotional turmoil, it is packed with opportunity for God to do a new and deeper work. How a congregation views and approaches the pastoral transition can be the difference between a healthy, successful transition and a repetition of a previous, unhappy experience.

There are three areas covered in this section: 1) the importance of congregational self-awareness; 2) the benefits of the intentional transitional model; and 3) the preparations needed before hiring a transitional leader.

Chapter 12

Congregational Self-Awareness

Congregations going through a pastoral transition often have certain common characteristics. Not every congregation in a pastoral transition has these characteristics, but many do.

Each characteristic described below, has a corresponding *best response*. These best responses are based on the experience of leaders who have helped congregations navigate the murky waters of a pastoral transition. The description of these characteristics shows what's normal during a pastoral transition, but also what's best.

Six Characteristics and Remedies for a Congregation in Transition

1. Loss has occurred — grieving is necessary.

The significance of a congregation's loss will vary from person to person and from congregation to congregation. In general, however, when a pastor leaves, there is an emotional connection lost. Some people will feel it ever so slightly, while others will feel it deeply and experience all the phases of the grief cycle.

> "He that lacks time to mourn, lacks time to mend."
> — William Shakespeare

The need for a congregation experiencing the loss of a pastor is time to grieve the loss. Grieving the loss includes holding off on entering into another long-term relationship with a new pastor before the grief process is complete. In the transitional model, this is called "closure." It is an indefinite period of time in which members are given various opportunities to walk through the grieving and letting go process.

2. An ending has come — a journey through the land between needs to follow.

After an ending takes place, the temptation is to rush forward towards a new beginning as soon as possible. Giving in to this temptation overlooks the value of having a time between an end and a new beginning.

It's not unusual for a congregation in transition to look ahead impatiently to the time when the next pastor will be found. Consciously choosing to camp out in the wilderness of loneliness and feed on the food God has supplied is hard work. The Israelites are an example of a people who needed to lean into their desert experience and allow God to transform them at a deep level before they were ready to enter the new land.

The "time between" is a ripe opportunity during which old ways of thinking, behaving, and operating can be exchanged for God's fresh new ways of thinking, living, and trusting. The Israelites struggled during their time between and often failed to trust and accept the wasteland as God's transformation school. They struggled to see the time between Egypt and the Promised Land as necessary. Yet God was

> "Before you can begin something new, you have to end what used to be. Before you can become a different kind of person, you must let go of the old identity. Beginnings depend on endings." — William Bridges

intent on using this time to transform them from immature, Egyptian-indoctrinated complainers into God-dependent worshipers with a whole new outlook on the world and God. Jeff Manion, in his book *The Land Between*, provides an excellent narrative of this journey.

3. A leadership vacuum has been created — stable interim leadership fills the void.

When the senior pastor leaves, a leadership vacuum is created. The vacuum needs to be filled. It is important for the congregation to develop an intentional plan to fill the vacuum and to fill the vacuum with the right kind of leadership. If a congregation waits too long or fails to come up with an intentional leadership plan, the situation may deteriorate and become more difficult to manage.

There are various places a congregation can look for help in dealing with this leadership vacuum. The congregation can call on denominational leadership, members of the staff, leaders from within the congregation, and transitional specialists from outside the congregation. More than likely, help will come from a combination of people. The right help makes a significant difference!

4. A loss of vision may have occurred — an opportunity to clarify the vision emerges.

Vision isn't always lost when a senior pastor leaves, but if it is, an opportunity exists to address this vision vacuum. Loss of vision may be because the leading champion of the vision is now gone. Vision may also be lost because the life cycle of the previous vision has ended. Either way, a need arises for the congregation to take a look at where it is and where it is going before it hires its next pastor.

One of the principles of change management is building a case for why the current vision and plan is no longer working. Without clear reasons for change and the urgency to do things differently, there won't be enough energy to discover God's new vision or implement a vision that is developed.

> "The past is important, but it is not nearly as important to your present as is the way you see your future." — Tony Campolo

141

A time of transition, with effective coaching and facilitation, can be a time when a congregation moves from vision uncertainty to vision clarity. It is also a time, if hearts are ready, when a congregation is in flux and able to embrace a renewed or new vision.

5. Loss of leadership creates insecurity — encouragement to trust Christ creates hope and strength.

If a congregation is too pastor dependent, the members may need a new perspective so that they can see themselves as the body of Christ with Christ as their head and leader. A new perspective may also include going from a place of insecurity without a leader to a place of renewed security in Christ. The willingness to trust the right transitional leader to guide them through their uncertainty can give members renewed spiritual strength.

Napoleon aptly stated, "Leaders are dealers in hope." A congregation in transition needs leadership to bring it hope, grounded not in wishful thinking but in God-directed plans and promises. A congregation in transition needs leaders to say, "Everything will be OK" — backed up with a plan to increase the chances of it being so.

6. Increased conflict and uncertainty do surface — godly, competent leadership brings reconciliation and hope.

Where the congregational culture allows spiritually immature people to grab hold of power, there is a need for solid leadership to step in. Denominational support and solid bylaws are not enough. Strong, on-site leadership is needed to deal biblically with inappropriate leaders who wish to take charge.

The best scenario is to put together a team of people who will work together to cover the various bases during a pastoral transition. A transitional leader can be part of the team and, if necessary, serve as the team leader.

Having a trained leader step into an unstable situation can close the leadership gap. If necessary, such a leader can map out a biblical process for dealing with destructive conflict and teach the congregation to engage in biblical peacemaking and productive conflict.

Reflective Questions

❖ What are some of the blinders a congregation wears that keep it from having healthy self-awareness during a transition?

❖ What aspects of the transitional process must be handled on an emotional level? How should that be accomplished?

❖ What parts of the transitional process need clear thinking and logic to deal with? How should that be facilitated?

Chapter 13

Understanding the Benefits

A congregation might lack the motivation to undertake a transitional journey. However, seeing the benefits of an intentional transitional ministry might convince the congregation to invest the time and trouble necessary to make such a process work.

Here are five benefits experienced when a congregation fully engages in an intentional transitional process:

1. The transitional model increases the likelihood of change.

Chapter 9 discussed the idea that when organizations are stable, they are frozen in equilibrium and cannot change until the equilibrium is somehow broken. For change to happen, three steps must be taken: 1) the frozen equilibrium has to be unfrozen; 2) the desired change has to be installed; and 3) the organism and organization have to be refrozen with the change in place.[36]

Congregational change is often difficult because people have made a significant investment to get to where they are and will not easily let go of that comfort to move to a new place. A calm period when a pastor is in place is not a very conducive time for adjustments to be made. The time between pastors, however, can be the crisis a congregation needs to force it to wake up, look in the mirror, and consider some change. Loren Mead puts it this way:

When pastors leave is indeed a moment of "unfreezing." It is a moment during which many of the forces holding the congregation immovable are loosened and opened up. It is a time at which the status quo can be questioned and explored without a sense of violation. When the pastor leaves a congregation, everybody knows instinctively that the old cannot be replicated in the same old way anymore—that some things will have to be faced and some done differently in the future. It does not determine *what* should be changed or *how* it should be changed; it merely asserts that the status quo is "in play." This is a time in which some things *can* change, if we choose to make it happen, as opposed to other times when things *might* happen, but generally do not.[37]

2. The transitional model opens the door to specialized help.

Many congregations find it financially challenging to bring in outside help during seasons of regular ministry. A pastoral exit, as difficult as it can be, frees up resources to pay for specialized help. There was no money for this when a lead pastor was being paid a salary even if the congregation could have used the outside help.

Since a congregation in transition is unfrozen and able to be changed, it makes sense that this is a perfect time to bring in someone who can make change happen. A trained and properly selected transitional leader can begin to deal with issues in the congregation that would otherwise be left untouched.

An outside transitional leader also brings skills and an outside perspective that can help to design a pathway towards greater health and vitality.

Outside help brings the needed objectivity and the push a congregation needs not only to see things differently, but also to act differently. Henry Cloud reinforces this idea in his book *Leadership Boundaries*:

Disorder and decline are not inevitable and can, in fact, be reversed if the system opens itself up to two things: a new source of energy and a template (a template is anything that serves as a guide, pattern, or model). You need force and you need the intelligence to inform action. If you have those two things, higher order functioning can take place. In a very tangible way, that is what leaders do when they pump energy and guidance into an organization or a team.[38]

3. The transitional model lowers anxiety for the search process.

The traditional or typical model says, "Our congregation will begin a search as soon as our pastor leaves—and transition will happen." The intentional transitional model says, "Our congregation will go into transition when our pastor leaves—and a search for the next pastor will begin at the right time during the transitional process."

A congregation that jumps into a search process before it is ready emotionally tends to *react* instead of *respond* to the vacuum created by the pastoral exit. Transitional ministry slows down the search process and allows it to flow naturally from a healthy place of the congregation knowing who it is and where it wants to go in the future. If the congregation doesn't take time to clarify its vision, it may send out a church profile describing the church it thinks it is, not the church it really is.

Profiles that present a false impression confuse and bewilder potential candidates. The future pastor should know who the congregation is and be in agreement with where it is going before coming to accept the pastoral assignment. If the pastor comes and is met with a completely different reality than was expected, it can lead to conflict and a premature exit.

4. The transitional model increases kingdom impact.

If a congregation has lost its sense of mission, has turned inward, and needs to adjust the way it goes about doing ministry, a rushed and unplanned transition will not allow enough time to correct the situation. Dealing with inconsistencies between who it wants to be and who it is can take a congregation months of conversation, prayer, and planning. The change won't be completed during the transition, but the foundation for future change can be established then.

The eight goals of the transitional model (see Section 2) are designed as milestones along the journey of transition. When the members and leaders of a congregation are all involved in the process, positive change is possible.

5. The transitional model provides a way to renovate and remodel.

A congregation can grow stale over time and lose its ministry effectiveness. This decline is natural as a congregation ages and moves from one stage of development to another. It doesn't, however, need to end there.

If a potential downward trajectory is recognized when a congregation is in a pastoral transition, it can be a flashing yellow light for the leaders and congregation. It is not a light that should create panic, but it is a warning that should be paid attention to. It should cause the leaders to say, "We will take ownership of this congregation. We will work alongside an effective transitional leader to figure out where we are and what needs remodeling and then start building a new foundation for the future. Once we get a sense of where God is leading us, we will find the right leader to take us there."

It's easier to renovate when a house is empty. A church isn't empty during a pastoral transition. It is, however, emptier at the leadership level. The time between pastors is an opportune time for putting out to pasture any sacred cows getting in the way of effective ministry and bringing into the open any elephants in the room that need to leave the building.

Reflective Questions

❖ Describe the difference between *features* and *benefits* in the intentional transitional model.

❖ What metaphors might help persuade a reluctant congregation to engage in an intentional transition?

❖ Which benefit speaks most loudly to you and why?

Chapter 14

Preparing the Congregation

Before a congregation can begin an intentional transition, some planning and preparatory work needs to be done. Included in the preparation is a preliminary self-assessment. This self-assessment will clarify the strengths and weaknesses, needs and resources of the congregation and assist in the selection of the right transitional leader. The congregation should also thoughtfully and carefully put together a transition team to work alongside the transitional leader.

Preliminary Self-assessment

Assessment is a core practice of transitional ministry. By doing a pre-assessment, a congregation is strengthening a muscle it will continue to exercise more fully when the transitional ministry begins. A pre-assessment will give a clear enough picture of the congregation to enable it to have an informed conversation about the kind of transitional leader it will need.

There are four areas to look at in this assessment:

1. The eight transitional goals

The pre-assessment rates the congregation in the eight goal areas of transitional ministry. The following chart gives a snapshot of the issues the self-assessment addresses. Like any assessment, the value is not in the numbers and written comments but in the

Area of Focus	Description
Closure	We need to work through a season of loss. We need to help people deal with past issues for the purpose of healing and closure.
Preaching	We need biblical truth communicated relevantly and practically. We need mature leaders to provide biblical messages.
Pastoral Care	We need to support and comfort those having difficulties in life. We need to mobilize caregiving within our congregation.
Administration	We need to organize people and programs for effective results. We need to delegate important responsibilities to other people. We need to further develop clear lines of communication.
Relationship Renewal	We need to experience spiritual renewal and passion for God. We need to connect with each other in meaningful ways. We need to connect with those not yet Christ-followers.
Vision Clarity	We need to discover God's vision and plan for the future.
Organizational Health	We need to analyze our systems and structures with the purpose of bringing about healthy change.
Search Process	We need a clear understanding of the type of senior leader who fits our unique situation.
Coaching One-on-One	We need help spotting and enlisting key leaders. We need help working with leaders one-on-one to encourage, support, and coach them.
Group Coaching and Facilitating	We need help facilitating and guiding the transitional process. We need help facilitating healthy meetings and conversations.

Table 2: Congregational Pre-assessment

conversation about what has been learned. The people who fill in the self-assessment are the key leaders who know the condition of the congregation.

2. Coaching and facilitation

The areas of coaching and facilitating have been added to the list of eight goal areas needing pre-assessment. The level of competency in these areas varies greatly from congregation to congregation. The key is for the leaders to know the strengths and weaknesses of the congregation in order to make use of the strengths that are there and to bring in people in the areas where the congregation is weak.

3. Needs and resources of the congregation

A slightly different angle is to prioritize the congregation's needs and consider the available resources. Resources include things such as people, leaders, finances, and denominational support.

Questions to consider include the following:

- What are the top five needs of our congregation at this time?
- Who are the resource people (e.g., staff, leaders, congregational members) we have currently in our congregation to help meet those needs?
- What kind of leadership do we need to bring in from the outside to help with our transition (e.g., coaching support, pastoral support, denominational support)?

4. The condition of the congregation in transition

There are at least three general descriptions of the condition of a congregation at the beginning of a transition. Which description fits a particular congregation will depend on the unique story of that congregation leading up to the transition. The common descriptions are:

- **A grieving congregation**

On one level, every congregation in transition experiences a season of grief since loss is part of every pastoral exit. But grief is the dominant characteristic of a congregation when the pastor has left after a season of fruitful ministry and the exit was not accompanied by serious turmoil, conflict, or negative circumstances. The pastor may be retiring, leaving for health reasons, moving into denominational ministry, or feeling called to another congregation for all the right reasons. An important truth to ponder during a relatively smooth transition is the need every congregation has to process grief, receive care, and experience healthy closure.

- **A traumatized or fractured congregation**

A traumatized or fractured congregation is often the result of a pastoral exit involving unhealthy conflict, a split, sexual infidelity at the leadership level, or some other crisis. In these cases, the traumatized emotional state of the congregation needs to be acknowledged and handled with extra care and attention. Specialized leadership is often required to untangle the mess and help navigate the unexploded land mines. What is needed is a leader who understands how to deal with wounded, angry, and possibly betrayed people.

- **An unfocused congregation**

An unfocused congregation needs to rediscover the unique focus God has for it. If a congregation has to look backwards to see the peak of its ministry effectiveness, it is time to refocus. If the community surrounding the congregation's ministry has changed and the congregation's ministry is no longer impacting the neighborhood, it is time to refocus.

Helping an unfocused congregation requires a certain kind of leadership. It requires a leader or a team of leaders who can have the right conversations, ask the right questions, and design the right process to fit the situation. The more stuck a congregation is, the deeper the change will need to be. It will help to ask questions such as these: Who are we? What are we here for? Who is our neighbor? But deep change is not usually linear. Going from unfocused to focused often requires a deeper shift in thinking, believing, and acting.

Choosing the Right Transitional Leader

Once a preliminary self-assessment has been done, it is time to begin looking for suitable leadership to help the congregation with the transition. Choosing a transitional leader is not as simple as hiring the first person who comes along. It requires diligence to match the right candidate with the unique needs and situation.

The following steps can help guide a congregation in the search for a suitable transitional leader. This list lays down general guidelines but is not exhaustive—a congregation should use it in partnership with other practices it has found effective in hiring.

Step 1: Identify who will conduct the search.

The first question to answer is: Who will search for and select the transitional leader? The search might be conducted by the board or by a team designated for that purpose. In some situations, the denomination might appoint a transitional leader or make recommendations about people who could be hired. There are also outside organizations such as Outreach Canada that can assist in the search for suitable candidates. Care should be taken to make sure everyone involved in the search is on the same page in terms of the philosophy and approach to take in the transition.

Step 2: Mobilize prayer for the search process.

Leadership selection is a spiritually discerned process and requires God's help and guidance. A mismatched or unqualified transitional leader will not provide the kind of leadership necessary to seize the opportunity buried within the transition. Prayer strengthens a congregation's dependence on God and opens up God's resources. Mark's Gospel records Jesus' promise:

> Have faith in God...Truly I tell you, if anyone says to this mountain, "Go, throw yourself into the sea," and does not doubt in their heart but believes that what they say will happen, it will be done for them. Therefore I tell you, whatever you ask for in prayer, believe that you have received it, and it will be yours. (Mark 11:22-24 NIV)

Step 3: Review the results of the preliminary self-assessment.

Once the group selecting the transitional leader is in place and prayer is mobilized, it is wise to review what was learned during the preliminary self-assessment. This review will bring to mind the issues and focus areas needing attention during the transition. It is also a good idea to develop a job description so a prospective transitional leader will know what his or her roles and responsibilities would be. Having a clear picture of the congregation brings greater clarity to the search. If a congregation doesn't know where it is going, it will be very challenging to find the right leader to help it get there!

Step 4: Develop a short list of potential transitional leaders.

Gathering names of suitable candidates is the next step in the search process. These names may come from a variety of sources and include specialists recommended by the denomination, people known by the congregation, transitional leaders in the area, leaders referred by a network, or people God brings across a congregation's path serendipitously. The search team should contact the potential candidates and ask for a resume summarizing their ministry experience and qualifications. The resumes can then be compared to the job description developed by the search committee. This will help the committee short-list the candidates and prepare for the interview process.

Step 5: Interview the candidates and check references.

Finding the right transitional leader increases a congregation's chances of having a fruitful transition. An important aspect of this is checking the candidates' references. The challenge is to find references who won't just tell the search committee what the candidate wants the committee to hear. Asking references for a reference is one way to drill down a little deeper.

When it comes to interviewing, there are various types of approaches. One is to include behavioral questions. This approach is based on the principle that "Past behavior is the best predictor of future performance." The following are some key behavioral questions to ask in the various areas of transitional ministry:

- **Closure:** Describe a time when you walked a congregation through a season of loss. What steps did you take to help the congregation heal and recover?
- **Preaching:** Tell us about a time you prepared a message to meet a perceived need. How did you discern the need, prepare the topic, and deliver the message?
- **Pastoral Care:** Tell us about a time you came alongside a group of people to provide pastoral care and shepherding. What did you do? Who did you do it with? What was the outcome?
- **Administration:** Give us an example of a time you took a mess and organized it in a way that brought clarity and order. What steps did you take? Give us the name of a person you delegated ministry to.
- **Relationship Renewal:** Give us your best example of a time you gave leadership to a congregation's spiritual renewal. Describe a time when you helped people become involved in a life of discipleship. Describe a time when you helped two people in conflict experience a repaired and reconciled relationship.
- **Vision Clarity:** Describe a time you walked a congregation through a vision clarification process. What steps did you take? What was the outcome? Who were the people you worked with, and what was your role in the process?
- **Organizational Health:** Tell us about a time you worked with a board to improve its spiritual health and its effectiveness. Describe the governance style you

are most comfortable with. When have you set aside your preferences to work with a group which had a different style from your own?

- **Search Process:** Give us your best example of how you helped a congregation with a pastoral search. What was your role in the process? What steps did you guide the congregation through?

- **Coaching One-on-One:** Give us the names of some people you have coached and mentored in the context of a leadership and ministry assignment. What did you do to develop and coach them? What was the outcome?

- **Group Coaching and Facilitating:** Describe a time you guided a group through a series of conversations resulting in greater understanding and ministry effectiveness.

Step 6: Hire the candidate, and set clear expectations.

Once the interviewing process has been completed and the best candidate has been selected, it is time to offer that person the job. That offer will likely result in some negotiation, as both sides try to reach agreement on the terms and conditions of the relationship.

Before any ministry partnership begins, it is important that expectations be clearly understood and written down. This can take the form of a signed agreement or contract plus a job description outlining the roles and responsibilities of the transitional leader. It is also necessary to clarify the expectations of the congregational leadership and the congregation. The parties involved need to know the length of the agreement, the process for renewing or terminating the agreement, the cost, the lines of authority and responsibility, the denominational involvement, and other details.

Building the Transitional Leadership Team

Another piece of the planning puzzle which will help the transitional process to begin well is to select the transition team before the transitional leader arrives. This will enable the transitional leader to hit the ground running.

The transition team is usually put together by the church board and reports regularly to the board throughout the transitional process. This team supports the transitional leader and helps him or her work as a partner of the congregation rather than as a lone ranger. The transition team should be composed of a cross section of people from the congregation, the leadership community, the board, and the staff.

John Kotter describes the key qualities of a transition team this way:

A powerful guiding group has two characteristics. It is made up of the right people, and it demonstrates teamwork. By the 'right people,' we mean individuals with the appropriate skills, the leadership capacity, the organizational credibility, and the connections to handle a specific kind of organizational change.[39]

For more on the transition team, see Chapter 21.

Reflective Questions

❖ How could the pre-assessment work better prepare a congregation for a season of intentional transition?

❖ What obstacles have you seen get in the way of properly preparing for an intentional transition?

❖ What characteristics would you include for the people serving on the transition team?

Section 4: The Transitional Leader

"The first responsibility of a leader is to define reality. The last is to say thank you. In between, the leader is a servant."

— Max DePree

At the heart of transitional ministry is competent servant leadership. Servanthood is the foundation on which spiritual leadership rests. Jesus embraced the life of a servant and showed the way:

When he had finished washing their feet, he put on his clothes and returned to his place. "Do you understand what I have done for you?" he asked them. "You call me 'Teacher' and 'Lord,' and rightly so, for that is what I am. Now that I, your Lord and Teacher, have washed your feet, you also should wash one another's feet. I have set you an example that you should do as I have done for you. Very truly I tell you, no servant is greater than his master, nor is a messenger greater than the one who sent him. Now that you know these things, you will be blessed if you do them." (John 13:12-17 NIV)

On that foundation rest the five necessary qualities of the transitional leader: character, competency, chemistry, capacity, and calling.

Chapter 15

Character

Who a leader is in private when no one is looking is who the leader really is. That is the leader's true character. Character is reflected in the words expressed by people after the leader has gone from the room or from the planet. Phillips Brooks said, "Character is manifested in the big moments, but it is made in the small ones." Abraham Lincoln said, "Character is like a tree and reputation its shadow. The shadow is what we think it is, and the tree is the real thing." This chapter describes some of the character qualities that it is important for a transitional leader to have.

Love

James Hunter describes the characteristics of a servant leader, based on the description of *agape* love in 1 Corinthians 13:

- **Patience** — showing self-control
- **Kindness** — giving attention, appreciation, and encouragement
- **Humility** — being authentic and without pretense or arrogance
- **Respectfulness** — treating others as important people
- **Selflessness** — meeting the needs of others
- **Forgiveness** — giving up resentment when wronged
- **Honesty** — being free from deception
- **Commitment** — sticking to one's choices[40]

Being a loving leader does not imply a soft sentimentality but a strong-hearted integrity and commitment to the best interests of others.

If we were to put the words of Paul in 1 Corinthians 13 into the language of leadership, they would read this way:

Leaders never give up. Leaders care more for others than for self. A leader doesn't want what he or she doesn't have. A leader doesn't strut, doesn't have a swelled head, doesn't force him or herself on others, isn't always "me first." A leader...doesn't fly off the handle, doesn't keep score of the sins of others, doesn't revel when others grovel, takes pleasure in the flowering of truth, puts up with anything, trusts God always, always looks for the best, never looks back, but keeps going to the end. (1 Corinthians 13 TM *modified*)

We are not born with these qualities but develop them as Christ works in us. Our part is to exercise the muscles of self-awareness and spiritual discipline while God does his part in growing these qualities within us to full maturity.

Self-awareness

A great deal of research confirms that IQ (intelligence quotient) and technical skills are far less crucial to leadership success than mature self-awareness. Self-awareness is part of EQ (emotional intelligence). Growth in self-awareness increases the ability to act and react appropriately in any given situation.

Chris Lowney said, "Leaders thrive by understanding who they are and what they value, by becoming aware of unhealthy blind spots or weaknesses that can derail them, and by cultivating the habit of continuous self-reflection and learning."[41]

Transitional situations are often chaotic, and plans will not be executed perfectly, so leaders in these situations require flexibility and adaptability. Self-awareness gives a leader the ability to see what is going on in enough time to respond rather than react.

Self-awareness was modeled by those in the Jesuit order. Ignatius of Loyola, the founder of the order, "essentially tore down the monastery walls to immerse his Jesuits in the maelstrom of daily life. Once those walls were down, Jesuits had to employ techniques to remain re-collected while all hell was breaking loose around them..."[42] Adapting on the fly and remaining "re-collected while all hell is breaking loose" is a critical skill for the transitional leader to possess.

Self-management is another side to self-awareness. Transitional leaders need the ability to see and feel what is going on inside themselves and to keep their emotions under control when their buttons are pushed or those around them are coming unglued. Self-awareness allows the transitional leader to respond as a non-anxious presence during anxious circumstances.

Balance

Another aspect of character is living a balanced life. Balance is something that can be observed from the outside, but it is only ever achieved by an inner commitment. General George S. Patton understood the role that self-discipline plays in maintaining a

> "Happiness is not a matter of intensity but of balance, order, rhythm and harmony."
> — Thomas Merton

healthy balance when he said, "Make the mind run the body. Never let the body tell the mind what to do. The body will always give up."

Balance is more like a journey than a destination. The idea is for the journey as a whole to be balanced, not to achieve perfect balance continually along the way. "Stuff happens" in life and ministry that throws people off balance, forcing them to grow and change until they once again find equilibrium.

When a person's life is out of balance, the following signs may appear:

- **Spiritual health** — dryness, alienation, serious doubt, holes in one's theology, limited spiritual resources

165

- **Emotional health** — unprocessed grief, secondhand pain, loneliness, ongoing depression
- **Intellectual health** — lack of fresh learning, limited new ideas generated through reading or interacting with others, using outdated sermons
- **Physical health** — ongoing illness, obesity, unhealthy eating habits, lack of sleep, lack of exercise, lack of recreation
- **Environmental health** — concern with one's living arrangements, too much clutter, repairs needed on a car or home, excessive debt, insufficient finances to meet needs
- **Relational health** — Marriage stress, unresolved conflict in family relationships or friendships, lack of a social life, too few friends

Working on ourselves from the inside out is never a quick or easy process, but it pays dividends well worth the investment. Stephen Covey said, "The greatest battles of life are fought out every day in the silent chambers of our own heart." Football coach Tom Landry stated: "To live a disciplined life and to accept the result of that discipline as the will of God—that is the mark of a man."

Spiritual Maturity

Character, for the Christ-follower, is forged through a process of learning and doing. This process of growth is sometimes hard but often filled with joy and the abundance Christ brings. All Christians begin as spiritual infants but are commanded by God to grow and become fully formed, mature followers of Jesus.

He handed out gifts of apostle, prophet, evangelist, and pastor-teacher to train Christ's followers in skilled servant work, working within Christ's body, the church, until we're all moving rhythmically and easily with each other, efficient and graceful in response to God's Son, fully mature adults, fully developed within and without, fully alive like Christ. No prolonged infancies among us, please. We'll not tolerate babes in the woods, small children who are an easy mark for impostors. God wants us to grow up, to know the whole truth and tell it in love—like Christ in everything. We take our lead from Christ, who is the source of everything we do. He keeps us in step with each other. His very breath and blood flow through us, nourishing us so that we will grow up healthy in God, robust in love. (Ephesians 4:11-16 TM)

Ruth Haley Barton, in her book *Strengthening the Soul of Your Leadership,* speaks of the growth process this way:

Spiritual transformation is the process by which Christ is formed in us for the glory of God, for the abundance of our own lives and for the sake of others...the transformation process...is an organic process that goes far beyond mere behavioral tweaks to work deep, fundamental changes at the very core of our being. In the process of transformation the Spirit of God moves us from behaviors motivated by fear and self-protection to trust and abandonment to God; from selfishness and self-absorption to freely offering the gifts of the authentic self; from the ego's desperate attempts to control the outcomes of our lives to an ability to give ourselves over to the will of God which is often the foolishness of this world. This kind of change is not something we can produce or manufacture for ourselves but it is what we most need. It is what those around us most need...the soul-full leader is faithful to the one thing he can do—create the conditions that set us up for an encounter with God in the places where we need it most. To continually seek God in the crucible of ministry no matter how hard it gets.[43]

Reflective Questions

❖ Which qualities in 1 Corinthians 13 are strengths in your life? Where do you need to see growth?

❖ Reflect on the qualities of a balanced life. If you think of the areas presented as the spokes of a wheel, which spoke in your life is weak or broken and needs attention?

❖ Write out your definition of a godly leader with sound character.

Chapter 16

Competencies

C ompetencies are those abilities or behaviors that enable people to do their jobs properly and effectively. Transitional leaders require a certain skill set to do their job with excellence. This skill set includes a broad range of general leadership skills but also some more specialized competencies.

It is important to differentiate between primary and secondary competencies. Primary competencies are those skills and abilities essential for doing transitional ministry. Every transitional leader needs, at the very least, a working understanding and ability to practice the primary competencies. Secondary competencies are those skills that are necessary occasionally but are not needed in every situation. Secondary competencies have a lesser impact on the transitional leader's overall effectiveness.

Primary Competencies

Leading

Leading is the ability to influence people to work enthusiastically towards agreed-upon goals and actions in order to reach a desired outcome. Leading is at the core of what it takes to guide a congregation from where it is to where God wants it to be.

The skill of leading is multi-faceted. It is, however, not out of reach for those willing to learn and grow. Peter gave these instructions to leaders:

I have a special concern for you church leaders. I know what it's like to be a leader, in on Christ's sufferings as well as the coming glory. Here's my concern: that you care for God's flock with all the diligence of a shepherd. Not because you have to, but because you want to please God. Not calculating what you can get out of it, but acting spontaneously. Not bossily telling others what to do, but tenderly showing them the way. (1 Peter 5:1-3 TM)

These words of Peter point back to character. Caring, unselfish, servant leaders understand certain principles and practices that set them apart from mediocre leaders.

The Five Practices	The Ten Commitments
Model the way	Clarify values by finding your voice and affirming shared ideals. Set the example by aligning action with shared values.
Inspire a shared vision	Envision the future by imagining exciting and ennobling possibilities. Enlist others in a common vision by appealing to shared aspirations.
Challenge the process	Search for opportunities by seizing the initiative and by looking outward. Experiment and take risks by constantly generating small wins and learning from experience.
Enable others to act	Foster collaboration by building trust and facilitating relationships. Strengthen others by increasing self-determination and developing competence.
Encourage the heart	Recognize contributions by showing appreciation for individual excellence. Celebrate the values and victories by creating a spirit of community.

Table 3: Five Practices and Ten Commandments of Leadership

According to *The Leadership Challenge*, there are five practices and ten commitments of sound and effective leadership.[44] These practices and commitments are indispensible for an effective transitional ministry. After all, "Everything rises and falls on leadership." (John Maxwell)

Coaching

Coaching is the ability to listen carefully, ask powerful questions, and guide the process of discovering God's agenda in order to bring it into reality. Coaching is more about asking than telling, more about being curious than having all the answers ahead of time, more about discovery than delivery. Solomon warned, "Don't jump to conclusions—there may be a perfectly good explanation for what you just saw." (Proverbs 25:8 TM) The "perfectly good explanation" is often spiritually discerned through the process of asking powerful questions and listening carefully for the answers. There are many skills required for coaching, but the three basic ones are an excellent place to start.

1. Listening

Listening is a form of leadership, as James says in his letter: "Lead with your ears, follow up with your tongue, and let anger straggle along in the rear." (James 1:19 TM) Listening, really listening, is being fully present with people so they feel heard and are able to untangle the thoughts that may be bouncing around in their heads. Listening is about paying attention to what another person is "really" saying, not just hearing the words coming out of his or her mouth.

"You've spent years learning how to read and write, years learning how to speak. But what about listening? What training or education have you had that enables you to listen so that you really, deeply understand another human being from that individual's own frame of reference?" — Steven Covey[45]

There are three levels of listening: 1) internal listening, where the attention is on ourselves and our own experience; 2) focused

171

listening, where the attention is on other people and their experiences; and 3) global listening, where the attention is on what's going on and what the Holy Spirit is saying in the situation. All three levels have their place in coaching, but levels two and three are most needed for effective coaching.

2. Asking powerful questions

Asking questions unlocks the discovery process for a person or a group of people. Chip Bell says, "Effective questioning brings insight, which fuels curiosity, which cultivates wisdom."

What's the value in asking questions instead of giving advice or telling someone what to do? Tony Stoltzfus explains that questions cause people to think, arrive at answers they believe in, and act on those answers. Asking moves people beyond passive acceptance of what others say to aggressively applying their creative ability to the problem at hand.[46]

There are two basic types of questions: open-ended and closed-ended. Open-ended questions give people a high degree of flexibility and freedom to respond. Closed-ended questions seek short, specific answers. Open-ended questions are helpful when the goal is self-discovery and exploration. Closed-ended questions are helpful when looking for facts or inviting people to make a commitment to a course of action.

> "I keep six honest serving-men, they taught me all I knew; their names are What and Why and When, and How and Where and Who." — Rudyard Kipling

3. Guiding the process

Guiding the process helps turn intention into action. If all the coach does is listen and ask questions without providing structure for the conversation, a critical component is missing, and coaching will not be effective.

Coaching is a change process summarized by the following equation: X → Y by Z. Change occurs when people

> The Coaching Equation:
> X → Y by Z

move from where they are (X) to where they want to be (Y) by doing something different (Z). "Sometimes the coaching equation comes to life from only one or two conversations, and sometimes the span of time is much greater because of the distance between X and Y or the scale of change involved in Z."[47]

To see how this works in practice, look no further than the process laid out in this book. The transitional process is a change journey designed to move a congregation from where it is (X) to where it wants to be (Y) by doing something different (Z). Guiding the process provides rails on which the energy of transition and change can travel to an agreed-upon destination.

Shepherding

Shepherding is the ability to provide loving pastoral support and care. It includes the ability to listen attentively and empathically to people. Shepherding helps people feel safe yet challenged to be all they can be. It is feeding and caring for people by giving them what they need, not just what they want.

A shepherding leader during a transition lets the congregation know two things: 1) everything is going to be OK— this lowers the anxiety level and lets people know someone is in charge; and 2) there is a plan in place to guide the congregation through the season of transition.

The degree and extent of the shepherding required during a transition will depend on the situation. In a highly wounded or stressed congregation, more specialized shepherding may be required. In a congregation where there is healthy community and a well developed system of care, shepherding may need less attention, especially from the transitional leader.

Facilitating

Facilitating is coming alongside a group of people to make their journey, process, or conversation easier or less difficult. To be a successful facilitator, there are things the transitional leader needs to *be* (qualities) and things the transitional leader needs to *do* (practices).

The qualities of a facilitator include:

- **Realistic optimism** — an attitude that believes God is at work in every situation even when things are difficult and that there is a way through the "stuff" in order to get to a new place
- **Non-anxious presence** — the ability to remain calm and peaceful even when the winds of change and chaos are blowing all around
- **Flexibility** — the quality of heart and mind that allows for fresh ideas, course corrections, and unanticipated outcomes
- **Loving truthfulness** — the ability to stand firm when necessary but with a heart of love and understanding. Leaders who speak the truth in love foster respect and trust in others.
- **Curiosity** — the ability to listen deeply, ask powerful questions, and keep wondering eyes wide open. A facilitator does not focus on telling people what to do but, through listening and asking questions, guides them to solutions and discoveries.

The following list is a sampling of some of the practices a facilitator could use:

- define group goals
- assess needs and learning gaps
- suggest and provide the appropriate tool or process
- guide the discussion
- test assumptions
- help people listen to each other
- use consensus building to help people make decisions
- help groups have difficult conversations
- provide feedback and reframe what's being said
- ask powerful questions
- stay neutral yet actively listen

Peter Senge summarizes the work of a facilitator with these words:

> Facilitators must continually bring forward people who have not spoken, and prompt them to add their views. They must regulate the flow of conversation, following a model of dialogue which invites people to suspend their assumptions and treat each other as colleagues. All the while, the facilitators must ask people to explain why they said what they just said—to urge them to describe what's behind their thinking.[48]

Managing Change

Managing change is the ability to facilitate a transition with an individual, team, or organization that helps them move from where they are to a desired future destination. Managing change is at the heart of the competencies required for leading a congregation during the time between pastors.

Change has many sides to it. Chapter 23 looks in more detail at the change process, but here we are looking at the leader who manages the change. Let's call that person the "change agent." To be effective change agents, transitional leaders must *be* before they will be able to *do*.

> "What we do flows from who we are."
> — Paul Vitale

Following are several qualities change agents need to have:
- Change agents need to be at peace with God, themselves, and others. Paul offered these words: "If it is possible, as far as it depends on you, live at peace with everyone." (Romans 12:18 NIV)
- Change agents need to be awake physically, emotionally, and spiritually. Only well-balanced, healthy people can be effective change agents.
- Change agents need to be attuned to the activity of God. They must be aware of where Christ is at work and where he is directing his people to go.

- Change agents need to be aware of themselves, the reality of others, and what's going on in the bigger picture. In other words, they need to possess emotional intelligence.

Flowing out of who change agents are to *be* are a number of practices change agents will *do*:

- A change agent forms a team. In order for change to run deep and last, it must be guided by a team of influential people within the congregation. The change agent's job is to partner with these key people to help navigate through the change process.
- A change agent finds wins to celebrate. As small changes are made during the change journey, the change agent helps the congregation celebrate small wins as they occur.
- A change agent fans the flame of urgency. Without urgency, change comes to a grinding halt. Urgency is the energy behind any change effort.
- A change agent facilitates numerous crucial conversations. Conversations that matter are not automatic or dictated from the front of the room or head of the table. They happen through a countless number of interactions facilitated by the skilled change agent.

Managing Conflict

Managing conflict is the ability to recognize and deal with differences in a rational, balanced, and biblical way through effective communication, problem solving, and biblical peacemaking practices.

Conflict is an opportunity to release creativity, challenge the status quo, develop leadership capacity, and unearth unhealthy patterns hindering ministry effectiveness. Conflict, on the

> How you manage conflict directly affects how others manage conflict with you.

other hand, can be destructive, harmful, and sinful. The difference between opportunity and destruction is the manner in which conflict is approached and managed.

A transitional leader can serve as a conflict coach, helping the congregation value the redemptive aspects of conflict, address past mismanaged conflict, and prepare for future conflicts. This is done by introducing new ways of thinking and acting when dealing with interpersonal and congregational conflict. A healthy and holy approach to conflict begins by understanding the dynamics of congregational conflict. It ends with modeling good conflict management and biblical peacemaking practices.

The starting point for helping the congregation to manage conflict successfully is for the transitional leader to understand his or her personal view of conflict and preferred approach to conflict. A transitional leader brings to a congregation a particular model for managing conflict, even if the transitional leader is unaware of it.

Following are three ways to increase the chances of success in managing conflict:

1. Conduct a conflict styles self-assessment.

Self-assessment will increase the transitional leader's understanding of the various conflict styles and the broad range of ways to deal with conflict. There are numerous assessment tools available, including those produced by conflict management specialists Ronald Kraybill, Speed B. Leas, and Jim Van Yperen.

2. Conduct a congregational assessment.

Some transitional leaders have a well-developed intuition when working with a congregation in conflict. Others tap into the grapevine to figure out what's really going on. In either case, it's always wise to test any assumptions gleaned through informal means with hard data.

The assessment methods could include interviewing, surveying, group forums, and note-taking while walking around.

Then the data should be put into a reviewable format and discussed with various groups within the congregation. The goal is to interpret the data and prayerfully discern what needs to be done as a result of the learning.

Once agreement is reached on the next steps to finding peace, the plan must be put into motion. Training the congregation in biblical peacemaking may be part of the plan since it increases the capacity of the congregation and its leaders to deal with conflict in a healthy way.

3. Continue growing in conflict management skills.

Leaders are learners. A transitional leader who wants to serve a congregation in the area of conflict and biblical peacemaking is no exception to this rule.

Training and resources abound for those seeking to grow in this area. A transitional leader does not need to become an expert in managing conflict, but gaining an amateur level of competency will be very useful. If the intensity of the conflict is too high, the transitional leader should not hesitate to invite other leaders more skilled in this area to facilitate the process.

Conflict in the church is never a surprise but is a natural byproduct of diversity. The goal is not to eliminate conflict, but to help the body stop reacting negatively to conflict and start turning conflict into an opportunity for God to do good. For more on managing conflict, see Chapter 24.

Communicating

Communicating is the ability to present ideas and information clearly and effectively through spoken and written words in positive or negative circumstances. Solomon pointed out the power of words: "Kind words heal and help; cutting words wound and maim." (Proverbs 15:3 TM)

Transitional leaders use words to guide and lead people. They use words in preaching, in speaking with people one-on-

one, and in group settings. Transitional leaders use the written word to communicate ideas, teach, and give direction to those they work with.

Spoken Communication

Andy Stanley described preaching this way:

But communication is: Here we all are. We all have a common need or desire. We all have something in common, and I am going to stay here until I make you feel the need to have it resolved. And then I am going to open God's Word and resolve it. And I am going to take that and tell you what you need to do specifically. And then I am going to take a minute and talk about what the world would be like, how much better off we would all be, if we would all do what the Scriptures say. It is really that simple.[49]

The context for communicating during a pastoral transition is determined by the phase a congregation is going through on any given week. It's important to preach on themes relevant to the issues and experiences of the congregation at that moment. The principle is to use the vehicle of spoken communication to stimulate biblical thinking, encourage faith, and foster godly living. This approach will help a congregation move from where it is to where God wants it to go.

Spoken communication goes beyond just preaching. Every interaction with staff, congregational members, and leaders is an opportunity to use words for the purpose of healing and helping.

Written Communication

Writing is a craft developed through practice, feedback, and more practice. The transitional leader has an opportunity, through written words (emails, blog posts, bulletin updates,

"The single biggest problem in communication is the illusion that it has taken place." — George Bernard Shaw

179

written summaries) to present ideas and concepts that people can use to make the transition easier.

Here are just a few places where written communication is required during the transitional process:

- correspondence between the congregation and the transitional leader before being hired
- agreements or contracts, where expectations are clearly laid out on paper for both parties to agree to
- a transitional blueprint, along with any communication needed for the congregation and leadership to understand and adopt the blueprint
- assessment documents that put into words the current reality of the congregation based on the data collected
- ongoing email correspondence between the transitional leader and the congregational leadership, denomination, and congregation
- documents used to train the congregation in matters relating to relationship renewal, vision clarity, and organizational health

Secondary Competencies

Secondary competencies are like hats the transitional leader is called upon to wear when a certain task needs to be done. They are tools in the transitional leader's toolbox that can be pulled out when needed. In some situations, a higher level of skill may be needed in a given area, but a general working knowledge of these competencies will serve the transitional leader well.

Administrator

A good administrator can bring order out of chaos, organize people, and work effectively with structures and systems. Depending on the size and complexity of the congregation and the gifting available in the congregation, this competency will be required in varying degrees.

The administrator role is secondary, not because it is unimportant, but because often the needed administrative gifts are already at work within the congregation. In some situations, a transitional leader will need a greater degree of administrative ability, which needs to be discerned by the congregational leadership before hiring the transitional leader.

Analyst

The analytical competency is the ability to gather and organize accurate information from an unbiased perspective and interpret that information in a meaningful way. It is the ability to listen, learn, and think carefully about what is really going on.

Being analytical is the foundation for effective problem solving. A problem solver sees all sides of a situation and thoughtfully assesses the value of each side before making a decision.

> "Leaders think and talk about the solutions. Followers think and talk about the problems."
> — Brian Tracy

Consultant

A consultant is a person who brings knowledge or expertise to a situation with the goal of helping to solve a problem. During a transition, there is an opportunity to bring a known solution into the conversation. However, the leader should avoid giving answers too quickly. It is wise for the transitional leader to give sufficient time for congregational self-discovery to occur through supportive coaching before the leader puts on the consultant hat.

> "Spoon-feeding in the long run teaches us nothing but the shape of the spoon."
> — E.M. Forster

As long as consulting doesn't drive the transitional process, it can serve a congregation well. Knowledge and expertise shared at appropriate times in the right manner can have a great impact. Transitional ministry is not a playbook to be followed line by line as much as it is a set of guiding principles to help a congregation and its leadership in its unique situation.

Entrepreneur

Entrepreneurship, according to Harvard Business School professor Howard Stevenson, is "the pursuit of opportunity without regard to resources currently controlled." Transitional leaders pursue opportunities by faith and find places where their services are needed. This means that transitional leaders should practice networking, self-promotion, and relationship building. They should put themselves in front of people to build trust and increase their chances of being invited to come and help. It is a dance between trusting God to open doors, and developing the skills to knock on those doors.

Mentor

Mentors share their experience, wisdom, and learning with others who are eager to learn and grow. Paul said to his mentee Timothy, "The things you have heard me say in the presence of many witnesses entrust to reliable people who will also be qualified to teach others." (2 Timothy 2:2 NIV)

> "Mentoring is: sharing life's experiences and God's faithfulness."
> — Janet Thompson

Mentoring can be both intentional and spontaneous. Mentoring will be natural for any transitional leader who has been growing and developing throughout life. The key is to see and seize mentoring opportunities.

Negotiator

A negotiator has the ability to dialogue with a person or group and arrive at a place of agreement after various opinions have been shared. The transitional leader negotiates with the congregation before starting an assignment and at various points throughout the transitional process. Quite often, a negotiator puts the negotiated agreements into writing. This ensures that what was agreed to is clear and that there is something tangible to fall back on in case of a later misunderstanding.

Team Leader

A team leader is someone who guides, directs, and gives leadership to a group of individuals working on a common goal or task. A leader uses skills such as listening, asking questions, and guiding the conversation to help a team of people move from where they are to where they want to get to. The level of competency a transitional leader has as a team leader will vary. Because of that, it's important to match the skill set of the transitional leader with the needs and expectations of the congregation.

Team Player

Being a team player is certainly one of the easier secondary competencies, but it is vitally important. Being a team player gives the transitional leader an opportunity to lead by example. As a servant leader, the transitional leader will be working with a team of people on a regular basis. Showing up with humility, curiosity, a willingness to serve, and a willingness to work with others will leave a lasting impression.

Reflective Questions

❖ As you review the list of primary competencies, what are your strengths and what are your growth areas?

❖ As you review the secondary competencies, what are your strengths and where are your weaknesses? Who could be a complementary partner?

❖ When you think about your own growth and development, where do you see yourself in one year? What's the first step in getting there?

Chapter 17

Chemistry

C hemistry is the intangible connection a transitional leader and congregation feel when they are at home with each other. Chemistry on its own is not enough to ensure a successful partnership, but it should not be overlooked either.

If a transitional leader has the skill set to do the work but does not mesh with the congregation in style and approach, their partnership could end up being far less effective. When a sports team brings a new player into its locker room, the team is not only concerned with talent but also with fit. The new player must be in sync with the culture and feel of the team.

There is a marked difference when fit is factored into the hiring process. Leadership expert Bill Hybels speaks about the importance of chemistry this way:

> I used to be a doubter when it came to emphasizing "fit" when hiring a new staff person. If they nailed the character requirement and had competence to spare, I was quite sure they would do fine. They'd learn to mesh with the existing team and me once they were on board. Not always so. I learned the hard way to trust my gut on this: if I get negative vibes the first two or three times I'm in someone's presence, it's likely I'm not going to enjoy working with that person day in and day out. Sounds crass, I know, but I have learned this painful lesson too many times.[50]

Benefits of Good Chemistry

There are several benefits to having chemistry between the transitional leader and the congregation:

- A good fit allows the transitional leader to gel quickly with the leaders and congregation. This allows the transitional work to begin with greater speed and urgency.
- A good fit reduces the level of tension and potential conflict, due to fewer differences and the likelihood that values will be more in alignment. With less tension, the ease of working together increases.
- A good fit leads to higher morale because of a greater connection emotionally and relationally.
- A good fit allows the ministry environment to be more enjoyable and creates a stronger desire for people to get involved. When morale is high, people are more likely to be in an optimistic and hopeful mood.

Where to Look for Chemistry

The Greek adage "Know thyself" is critical in determining the right fit. The transitional leader needs to be self-aware, as does the congregation.

There are four areas to consider when potential transitional leaders evaluate who they are in ministry and where they fit. Though not exhaustive, the following list includes the main categories.

1. Leadership style

Leaders come in all shapes and sizes. Leadership style has to do with how the transitional leader approaches and works with people.

Glen Blickenstaff describes the four basic leadership styles as directive, participative, laissez-faire, and adaptive. [51] When transitional leaders know their dominant style, they will be able to assess what is required and whether they will be compatible with the congregation they are looking to work with. Similarly, the congregation needs to identify the style of leadership best suited to its situation.

2. Philosophy of ministry

Philosophy of ministry covers several aspects of leadership, including behavior, practice, belief system, value set, and attitudes. The way the transitional leader approaches ministry needs to match the way the congregation approaches ministry. For example, if the transitional leader is a strong proponent of "the purpose-driven church" or is radically "missional," that leader will need to find a congregation that is like-minded or that desires to move in that direction.

3. Personality

Leaders and congregations have personalities, and it is crucial that those personalities are compatible. The classic historical temperaments are *sanguine* (pleasure-seeking and sociable), *choleric* (ambitious and leader-like), *melancholic* (analytical and thoughtful), and *phlegmatic* (relaxed and quiet).[52]

Knowing their personality type will help transitional leaders assess the kind of situations they are best suited for. Similarly, a congregation that can assess its own personality is better equipped to find a suitable transitional leader. If, for example, a congregation wants a cheerleader and charismatic transitional leader, it won't want to hire an analytical, thoughtful person—and a wise laid-back introvert won't want to apply.

4. Personal preferences

Personal preferences include a whole range of beliefs and practices. All successful people have learned to accept and overlook differences. However, transitional leaders must know the areas where they are unable or unwilling to compromise. For example, a leader with an unwavering belief in a specific approach to church governance should not consider a partnership with a congregation that holds to a different governance model and is not seeking to change.

Some Final Thoughts on Chemistry

The principle that undergirds the need for chemistry is that transitional leaders will fit best where they can honor and respect the beliefs and practices of the congregation. If a congregation decides it wants to go in a different direction and the transitional leader has the ability to facilitate the change, the differences will serve as stepping stones. If the congregation is unwilling to change, the differences will be stumbling blocks.

Both transitional leaders and congregations should spend some time reflecting on questions pertaining to chemistry.

Transitional leaders should ask themselves these questions:
- What is my dominant leadership style (directive, participative, laissez-faire, or adaptive)?
- How would I describe my philosophy of ministry? What is my preferred church governance model? How should the church do evangelism? What's the role of the laity in the church? What's the role of the pastor? What's my style of preaching?
- What is my personality type? What does that mean when applied to ministry? How well can I style shift when necessary?
- What are my non-negotiables in terms of leadership, theology, and practice? What am I willing to overlook?
- What personal preferences should I keep in mind when considering a ministry opportunity?

Congregations should ask themselves these questions:
- What type of leader does our congregation need and want (directive, participative, laissez-faire, or adaptive)?
- What is our philosophy of ministry? How would we describe our church governance model? How do we

practice evangelism? What's the role of the laity? What style of preaching do we prefer?

- What is our basic personality as a congregation?
- What are our non-negotiables in terms of leadership, theology, and practice?
- We have decided to make a shift in style and focus. What leadership qualities will a transitional leader need to help us make that change?

Reflective Questions

❖ What would you add to the list of benefits when there is good chemistry?

❖ If you are a transitional leader, write a paragraph describing yourself in terms of chemistry and ministry fit.

❖ When in your experience have you seen bad chemistry? What was the result?

Chapter 18

Capacity

C apacity is the level at which a person is able to perform certain duties. It's also the degree to which a person can carry the responsibilities associated with a given situation. In considering a transitional ministry assignment, a leader not only needs the right competencies, but also adequate experience, the proper gift mix, the right skill set, the necessary physical and emotional strength, and the ability to make the position work geographically.

It is important for transitional leaders to honestly assess their capacity before agreeing to step into an assignment. Here are two examples to help illustrate what capacity is all about:

Congregation #1: A large urban congregation of 2,500 has a multi-staff, multi-layered organization. A potential candidate for transitional leader has only worked with two congregations in transition, and both of them were under 250 in size. Based on experience, this leader might not have the capacity to handle this position.

Congregation #2: A congregation, located in a city 2,000 miles away, has called a potential leader to come and help with a transition. The leader is excited because the congregation is part of the same denomination, and the leader knows he has the skill set, character, competency, and chemistry to help the congregation. The catch is that the leader's 16-year-old son is struggling in school and is experiencing emotional problems requiring a considerable amount of the leader's time and energy. If the leader takes on a ministry assignment away from home right now, his son will not receive the support he needs, and the burden will be too great for his wife to handle on her own. The leader should say no because he does not have the capacity for this assignment at this time.

Categories to Help Define Capacity

There are five categories useful for assessing capacity. The following list of categories is not exhaustive but is designed to stimulate thinking and provide solid direction for assessing capacity.

1. Emotional health

Transitional ministry is emotionally draining work. The transitional leader is dealing with change, building new relationships, traveling, and spinning various plates simultaneously. The leader might also have the added financial pressure that comes from accepting short-term assignments and having no guaranteed "next church" waiting when an assignment is over.

A leader needs the emotional strength and energy to withstand the pressure of transitional ministry. A leader on the verge of burnout and exhaustion won't be effective. Depleted and weary leaders who feel called to this work should first take time out to rest and recharge their depleted batteries before stepping into the arena of transitional ministry.

2. Family

Family demands and interests will determine availability and capacity for transitional ministry. The age of the leader's children affects availability and portability. Family finances need to be solid enough to handle short periods of time when the leader is without a ministry assignment or waiting for the next ministry assignment to begin.

The leader and the leader's spouse need to be "singing off the same song sheet" when it comes to transitional ministry. Whether the spouse goes with the leader to the congregation or stays at home and is plugged into a home church, they need to be in agreement on accepting the position.

3. Experience

Experience is a key factor in a leader's ability to step into a transitional assignment with confidence. The leader's experience needs to be suited to the size and complexity of the congregation.

If leaders would like to increase their capacity, it is wise for them to take baby steps in the direction they'd like to go. They can increase their capacity through coaching, mentoring, or professional development. They should not, however, pretend they are farther along than they are and take on a situation that is over their heads. If they do, they'll be frustrated and stressed and will fail to provide the leadership that is needed.

4. Geography

Where they live can affect the reach of transitional leaders. There are some transitional leaders who are entirely available to travel and work over a broad geographical area. They give a modern meaning to the old idea of "itinerant ministry."

Most leaders involved in transitional ministry have a home base from which they operate. If the congregation they're working with is an easy commute from their home, geography won't be an issue. If, however, the assignment is out of commuting range, they will need to negotiate their travel, work in blocks of time (e.g., two weeks on and one week off), or move to temporary accommodations in that location. A long-distance assignment also must be in harmony with family needs and other commitments.

5. Culture

"Culture" describes certain characteristics of a congregation such as language, history, social habits, music, tradition, and ethnicity. To have "cultural capacity," a transitional leader must have the sensitivity, understanding, and mindset required to build trust and lead a particular congregation. Transitional leaders with cultural capacity are aware of who they can work with and who they cannot work with culturally.

Questions to Ask

Here are some questions transitional leaders should ask themselves to help assess their capacity:

- How would I rate my emotional health? Are there any signs of burnout or fatigue I need to pay attention to?
- What are the needs of my family that affect my ability to be involved in transitional ministry? How does my spouse feel about my involvement in this kind of ministry? What is my financial situation? Do I have the capacity to live with periods of time when there is no paycheck?
- How would I describe my experience in terms of the kind of congregation I feel capable of leading? What is the range in terms of size of congregation I am equipped to serve, based on my experience? What does my experience say about my capacity to work with smooth, rough, or crisis transitions?
- What is my geographical range? Will I need to work within driving distance of my home, or am I willing to travel a distance to work with a congregation in transition?
- What parameters would I put on my capacity to work with different cultural realities? What are my unique qualifications in terms of language, ethnicity, background, and history?

Reflective Questions

❖ How would you assess your capacity in the five capacity categories?

❖ What would help you increase your capacity (e.g., coaching, training, mentoring, observation)?

❖ What is a congregation's role in discerning the capacity of a prospective transitional leader?

Chapter 19

Calling

To be effective in transitional ministry, God's call is essential. Transitional ministry is not just a job but an expression of the grace of God working through the transitional leader to impact people. Frederick Buechner says, "The place God calls you to is the place where your deepest gladness and the world's deepest hungers meet."

The call to transitional ministry is an invitation to listen for and respond to God's voice. It flows out of a life surrendered to God. Solomon advises, "Trust God from the bottom of your heart; don't try to figure out everything on your own. Listen for God's voice in everything you do, everywhere you go; he's the one who will keep you on track." (Proverbs 3:5-6 TM)

A Call Starts with the Universal Call

The unique call to transitional ministry flows out of the universal call all Christ-followers respond to. Os Guinness describes the universal call this way: "Calling is the truth that God calls us to himself so decisively that everything we are, everything we do, and everything we have is invested with a special devotion, dynamism, and direction lived out as a response to his summons and service."[53]

Paul ends his first letter to the Thessalonians with a vision of what God calls people to become:

May God himself, the God who makes everything holy and whole, make you holy and whole, put you together —

spirit, soul, and body—and keep you fit for the coming of our Master, Jesus Christ. The One who called you is completely dependable. If he said it, he'll do it! (1 Thessalonians 5:23-24 TM)

The Call to Transitional Ministry Is also Unique

The call to transitional ministry takes the universal call one step further. It includes a Holy Spirit-led directive to step into a leadership role with a congregation experiencing a time between pastors.

The particular focus of this call may vary. A call may focus on the ministry of reconciliation, congregational renewal, transformation, or temporary shepherding. A call may be rooted in the leader's burden to help struggling members in a congregation move from hopelessness and despair to renewed hope and a new beginning.

There is no "one way" God's calling is expressed for every leader. What is consistent is a renewed energy and passion to step into a place where the leader's gifts, abilities, and competencies are combined with God's Spirit at work within the leader.

The following words, addressed to pastors in *The Heart of a Great Pastor,* apply to those called to transitional ministry as well:

A robust, up-to-date call energizes all phases of ministry. A call invigorates the person who is called and makes him spiritually alive. It sharpens his focus on the meaning of his ministry. It makes him more noble and more in touch with God than he could have ever been without it. It vitalizes vision and fuels motivation. And a call reserves a front-row seat for a pastor at what resurrection life does for human beings.[54]

Being in a place God has not called the leader to looks very different: "A low-intensity call always leads to arid deserts of unsatisfying service...a disconnection from our call damages ministry fully as much as shutting off oxygen damages the brain or as withholding nourishment weakens the body."

Biblical Examples of Being Called

There are as many different ways God calls leaders into his service as there are leaders. Looking at the experience of a few leaders from the Bible will illustrate this.

Nehemiah

Nehemiah's call was to go and help God's people rebuild the broken walls of Jerusalem. This call does not appear to have been a direct command from God but rather was birthed out of Nehemiah's compelling desire to help his friends in crisis:

> Those who survived the exile and are back in the province are in great trouble and disgrace. The wall of Jerusalem is broken down, and its gates have been burned with fire. When I heard these things, I sat down and wept. For some days I mourned and fasted and prayed before the God of heaven. (Nehemiah 1:3-4 NIV)

After Nehemiah prayed and traveled around the city at night to survey the damage, he took the next step—he went back to the king and, with the Lord's help, made a risky request:

> The king said to me, "What is it you want?" Then I prayed to the God of heaven, and I answered the king, "If it pleases the king and if your servant has found favor in his sight, let him send me to the city in Judah where my ancestors are buried so that I can rebuild it." Then the king, with the queen sitting beside him, asked me, "How long will your journey take, and when will you get back?" It pleased the king to send me; so I set a time. (Nehemiah 2:4-6 NIV)

God was in Nehemiah's transitional assignment. God found him to be a willing partner in his work of rebuilding a broken city and bringing hope to a demoralized people.

Moses

The call of Moses to lead God's people through their transition from slavery to freedom came through the burning bush. Moses' call to lead was preceded by decades of preparation and culminated in a dramatic encounter with God.

"And now the cry of the Israelites has reached me, and I have seen the way the Egyptians are oppressing them. So now, go. I am sending you to Pharaoh to bring my people the Israelites out of Egypt." But Moses said to God, "Who am I that I should go to Pharaoh and bring the Israelites out of Egypt?" And God said, "I will be with you. And this will be the sign to you that it is I who have sent you: When you have brought the people out of Egypt, you will worship God on this mountain." (Exodus 3:9-12 NIV)

We don't always agree with what God is calling us to do. Moses didn't initially want to accept God's call due to his sense of inadequacy. He did, however, eventually relent and step into the challenging opportunity God called him to. Saying yes to God's call may not be easy, but it results in the deep satisfaction of being in the middle of God's will. God even met Moses part way and provided a spokesman to help him in the area of his insecurity.

Paul

Paul's call as a follower of Jesus began with a dramatic encounter with a bright light on the Damascus Road. When Saul asked who was speaking to him, a voice replied, "I am Jesus, whom you are persecuting. Now get up and go into the city, and you will be told what you must do." (Acts 9:5-6 NIV)

Paul's dramatic conversion was followed up by mentoring, personal growth, and specific instructions for the work Paul was to do. Several times Paul was guided specifically into areas of service. At one point, his plan to take the message of Jesus to Asia was blocked, so he backed off. Eventually, a call came to take the gospel to Macedonia:

> That night Paul had a dream: A Macedonian stood on the far shore and called across the sea, "Come over to Macedonia and help us!" The dream gave Paul his map. We went to work at once getting things ready to cross over to Macedonia. All the pieces had come together. We knew now for sure that God had called us to preach the good news to the Europeans. (Acts 16:9-10 TM)

> Being "led into" a ministry assignment is a frequent occurrence in Scripture. It involves a person with the right skill set, gift mix, and character encountering some form of human need that the person can meet with God's help and power.

Some Final Thoughts

Responding to the call of God involves a life of prayer, listening, and obedience. It's not about sitting around and waiting for the phone to ring but about "actively waiting." It involves knocking on doors, connecting with people, continuing to grow, and then being ready to walk through when a door opens.

There are multiple ways God calls his servants into ministry. People who are looking for one specific way and formula won't find it here. What is here is the encouragement to abide in Christ and allow God's Spirit to reveal his will and purpose. Remember that "The place God calls you to is the place where your deepest gladness and the world's deepest hungers meet." (Frederick Buechner)

Reflective Questions

❖ How do you describe God's call in a Christian's life? How do you describe God's call in your life?

❖ As a transitional leader, how are you sure God has called you into this particular ministry?

❖ What biblical example do you resonate with when thinking about God's call to ministry leaders?

My Call to a Transitional Assignment

When presented with an opportunity to serve as a part-time transitional leader, I wrestled with God over whether or not I should actually do it. I resisted the opportunity, even though I knew I could do the work. I just wanted to make sure it was God's assignment for this season of my life. I didn't just want the board of the church to call me but the Lord to call me.

While reading Jeremiah 1 and praying for direction, I received my answer very clearly. I sensed in that moment that the words were directed to me: "But you — up on your feet and get dressed for work! Stand up and say your piece. Say exactly what I tell you to say. Don't pull your punches or I'll pull you out of the lineup. Stand at attention while I prepare you for your work. I'm making you as impregnable as a castle, immovable as a steel post, solid as a concrete block wall. You're a one-man defense system against this culture, against Judah's kings and princes, against the priests and local leaders. They'll fight you, but they won't even scratch you. I'll back you up every inch of the way." (Jeremiah 1:17-19 TM)

This word to Jeremiah became God's word for me. It helped me step into this assignment knowing God wanted me to participate with him in it. The call kept me going through tough meetings and hard conversations. I also experienced moments of joy and meaningful ministry.

At the end of the assignment, I felt satisfied because I had done the work for a greater Master. I was also able to leave the congregation in the capable hands of the next leader, knowing I had completed my God-given assignment.

— Cam Taylor

An Unexpected Call to Transitional Ministry

My call to transitional ministry came after 11 years of pastoral ministry. Earlier in my life, at the age of 22, God had called me into pastoral ministry, but, due to my disobedience, I had chosen another path.

In 1997, while I was in Manila, the Philippines, on a three-week, short-term mission, God (the Hound of Heaven) reminded me that while I still had life, I needed to surrender to his will. Upon my return and after much prayer and discussion with my wife and family, I began the process of completing my training.

The year I turned 60, I graduated from Bible school and was ordained. I served as an associate pastor for 11 years, but the position was reduced to half-time due to financial concerns. It was then, as I served alongside an intentional interim pastor, that I received the encouragement and support from him and the church to pursue training for intentional interim ministry.

It has been a real blessing to have been involved in my first intentional interim assignment and to see God use the years of business experience, practical experience, and ministry experience to enable me to come alongside a church in transition. With so many churches in transition, I can see clearly how God has raised up this ministry "for such a time as this." It is my joy and privilege to be able to serve in this important work.

— Bruce Sticklee

Section 5: The Transitional Plan and Process

"Before you can begin something new, you have to end what used to be. Before you can become a different kind of person, you must let go of the old identity. Beginnings depend on endings."

— William Bridges

Intentional transitional ministry requires planning. The road traveled to develop a plan is paved by hard work, dedication, wise leadership, and prayer on the part of those responsible for guiding the transitional process. Those responsible include congregational leaders, denominational representatives (if it is a denominational church), key congregational members, and the transitional leader.

This section discusses several principles and practices important to the transitional process. It also discusses the nuts and bolts of developing and working with the transition team. Chapter 22 discusses the development of a transitional blueprint. Chapters 23-25 discuss three "must know" areas: leading change, managing conflict, and facilitating the model.

Chapter 20

Beginning Well

A congregation's transition between pastors begins officially the day the pastor leaves. Unofficially and emotionally, the transition begins the moment the pastor announces his or her exit. The focus in this section is on the official transition, from the point at which a transitional leader is hired and begins giving leadership to the transitional process.

There are several guiding principles presented here as a framework on which to hang ideas and purposeful activities. Each principle plays out differently in different situations, but together they provide a general guide for the season of transition.

10 Principles for Beginning Well

Principle 1: Build a team

"Teamwork makes the dream work," as John Maxwell so aptly states. The dream of a healthy, transformative transition becomes a reality when people work together from a place of trust and mutual respect.

To make the transitional dream work, a transition team is needed. The team is usually established by the church board and serves alongside the board as a partner in the transitional process. The team also works in cooperation with the transitional leader. The team members are the hands, feet, eyes, ears, and voice of the transitional process. The team must contain sufficient people with the credibility, skill, connections, reputation, and influence to provide strong leadership and make change happen.

Principle 2: Write a plan

"Careful planning puts you ahead in the long run; hurry and scurry puts you further behind." (Proverbs 21:5 TM) The planning for the transitional process begins as soon as it is known that a transition will take place. The planning should outline with broad brush strokes the transitional goals and establish rough timelines and milestones for the journey. However, things will inevitably change. Because of that, it's wise to understand the plan as a guide that will need to be adjusted as the congregation moves through the various phases of the transition.

Principle 3: Assign duties

Once the initial plan is in place, it is time to answer the question: Who will do what by when? No plan can be implemented until responsible people say yes to it and follow through with action. Duties can be delegated to any number of people within the congregation. The key is to have a responsible person in charge of each task and a way to report progress on the assigned task back to the transition team.

Principle 4: Mobilize prayer

Prayer is essential in order for deep change to occur. A congregation living in the center of God's will makes prayer a priority. God's Word powerfully promises, "If my people, who are called by my name, will humble themselves and pray and seek my face and turn from their wicked ways, then I will hear from heaven, and I will forgive their sin and will heal their land." (1 Chronicles 7:14 NIV)

Prayer and humility open the door to a two-way dialogue between people and God. William McGill said, "The value of consistent prayer is not that he will hear us, but that we will hear him." As prayer

> "Work as if it all depends on you. Pray as if it all depends on God." — Saint Ignatius

is practiced throughout the transitional process, it reinforces a dependence on God and results in divine power being made available for the hard and challenging work of transition.

Principle 5: Stabilize ministry

Regular weekly ministry must go on during the time between pastors. Beginning well involves figuring out how ongoing ministry will be provided.

There's an advertisement that shows a plane being remodeled while carrying passengers in mid-flight. It's hilarious but a wonderful metaphor for transitional ministry. Transitional leaders don't have the luxury of landing the plane and working quietly in the hangar before taking off again. They have to figure out how to renew and repair the congregation while it stays in the air. Doing that is both a skill and an art.

Principle 6: Prepare tools

Transitional ministry requires an array of ministry tools. Tools are needed for assessment, for closure, for facilitating crucial conversations, for resolving conflict, for team building, and much more. Gathering tools is something that should be done from the beginning of the transitional process.

Tools come from a variety of sources: the transitional leader, the denomination, the congregation and its leadership, and other resourceful people and organizations. Agreement is needed on which tool to use and when to use it. It is also important that the person using the tool is skilled enough in its use to achieve the desired outcome.

Principle 7: Hear stories

Transitional leaders should start listening right away to the story of the congregation. The story might be sad, disappointing, or joyful. The point in the beginning is not to fix problems, judge, or draw conclusions. The point is to listen and gather the common themes and plot lines that make up the big story.

The story is learned through talking to individuals and facilitating conversations in groups. Certain stories are group appropriate, while others need to be told in private and handled appropriately. As the stories are told, over time they build a body of knowledge and understanding that becomes useful in assessment and data collection.

Principle 8: Begin closure

There is no telling how long closure takes in any given congregation. It depends on several factors: the depth of the loss, the presence or absence of trauma, the openness of the people, and the influence of unresolved events from the past.

> "In the space between chaos and shape there was another chance."
> — Jeanette Winterson

What is universal in every congregation is the need to facilitate an ending and a letting go of the past. The readiness for closure increases as the congregation grows in its awareness of its emotional journey. Beginning well includes putting into place events, structures, and opportunities to help people move through the stages of grief.

Principle 9: Communicate often

Communication is a foundational building block of transitional ministry. Communication has many faces: a well-crafted sermon, a clearly written email update, a well laid out presentation given at an information meeting, or a phone call explaining the progress of the transition to a key influencer.

Regular communication lowers anxiety and keeps people aware of the progress being made throughout the transitional process. When people are given the right information, unhealthy gossip dries up, and morale rises.

> "The two words 'information' and 'communication' are often used interchangeably, but they signify quite different things. Information is giving out; communication is getting through."
> — Sydney J. Harris

Principle 10: Evaluate regularly

During the transition between pastors, change is constant. For this reason, frequent assessment and evaluation are essential. Evaluation helps the transitional leader recalibrate, to see where "here" is on the way to "there." The transition team needs to build evaluation into its meetings so it can keep the transitional process moving and regularly report progress to the congregational leaders and the congregation.

Reflective Questions

❖ Why is beginning well so important in transitional ministry?

❖ What mistakes have you made or witnessed in the early stages of a transitional process that came back to disrupt the process later?

❖ What principle would you add to the ten principles for beginning well listed here?

Introducing the Transitional Process

This week, the transition team begins its work of prayer, planning, and facilitating. The transition team has been put in place by the board to serve our congregation and help guide us through a spiritually discerned process of pastoral transition. Our goal during this time is to gain greater health, maintain effective ministry, and prepare well for the entrance of a new senior pastor in the timeframe God intends.

Studies show that when there is a change of pastors, there are varying degrees of awareness and impact. There are also a multitude of conflicting ideas about how to navigate the time between pastors. We are beginning our transition by seeking to gain a deeper understanding of where we've been and what we're experiencing emotionally, and by bringing closure to the past. Only then will we be able to start a dialogue about what's next.

Change happens, but transition is a process. This is true in every arena of life. Take, for example, the changes that occur when you sell your house. You sell your house, but then you have to sort, toss, and pack. Then you move, unpack, and reinvent yourself in the new place. Each family member experiences the change from his or her own unique emotional and practical perspective. The journey through transition to the new life is a shared experience on one level, but an individual journey on another.

Congregations are like families. When change happens, we have different feelings about the change. As we begin our transition, we want to give permission to you, the members of our congregation, to take this transition at your own pace. We, the leaders and transition team, are here to help make your trip possible and to help you avoid getting stuck and unable to move on. Together, let's ask God to help us understand our emotions around the changes taking place and give us courage for the journey of transition ahead.

– The Transition Team

Chapter 21

Building a Team

O ne of the first priorities when beginning the transitional process is to form a transition team. This team is necessary to support the process and partner with the transitional leader. Where the team members are found varies from congregation to congregation. What's key is that the members are spiritually mature, emotionally healthy team players.

The demands on this team will be high, but their investment will be well worth it. Paul Harvey described working together as a team this way: "The spirit of interdependence will not cost us more than it's worth. On the steep slope ahead, holding hands is necessary. And it just might be that we can learn to enjoy it."

What Is a Team?

A team is built on the qualities of trust, respect, productive conflict, agreed-upon action, accountability, and tangible results. Walter C. Wright defines a team this way: "A team is a small group of people working together on a common objective, dependent upon one another's contribution, knowing each other's strengths and weaknesses, caring about each other's growth and development, and holding one another mutually accountable."[55]

A team can accomplish more than a group of individuals working independently because of the synergy they have as a team. A single draft horse can pull a load of up to 8,000 pounds, but two draft horses hooked together can pull, not 16,000 pounds, but 24,000 pounds.[56] That is the power of teamwork!

There are three elements needed for teams to succeed: a task to accomplish, healthy relationships, and a process to follow. In transitional ministry, the task is to complete the eight goals of transitional ministry. But the goals cannot be achieved without fostering healthy team dynamics throughout the team's life. The process is the map outlining the journey the team and the congregation will travel during the transition.

Figure 14: Elements of Team Success

The People on the Transition Team

The transition team can be assembled in a variety of ways. In a smaller congregation, the leadership board might add the work of the transition team to its responsibilities. In medium to larger congregations, a separate transition team might be appointed by the leadership board but report to and work under the leadership board.

Here are a few principles to keep in mind when selecting a team:

- Include on the team key influencers from both the leadership community and the congregation.
- Select team members from a cross section of the congregation, not just from one demographic or age group.
- Select people who are good team players and on board with the direction of the congregation.
- Avoid people who have their own agenda, are overly dominant, or have a track record of being toxic when working on a team.
- Include people from various ministry areas to help break down any silos that may exist dividing departments or ministries.

Complementary Strengths of an Effective Team

When assembling a transition team, it is important to find people with certain skills and competencies or the potential to develop these skills and competencies. It's also normal for certain team members to possess more than one of these competencies. People are needed on the team to fill the following roles:

- **Leader** — the leader serves the team and is instrumental in recruiting, guiding the process, moving the team toward functionality, and helping it arrive at the desired result.
- **Doer** — the doer gets the work done by taking instruction and serving as the legs, feet, and hands of the team.
- **Organizer** — the organizer takes the ideas and plans of the team and helps put them into a workable format and timetable.
- **Relater** — the relater pours oil on relationships, builds community, and reminds people to enjoy the journey and care about each other.
- **Innovator** — the innovator provides new ideas and insights to help the group look outside the box for solutions and options.
- **Analyzer** — the analyzer asks hard questions and challenges ideas in order to make what's mediocre better.
- **Writer** — the writer puts into words what the team wants to keep a record of or communicate in writing to others.
- **Liaison** — the liaison has good rapport with those outside the system but who need to be on board with the vision and plan.

The Basics of an Effective Transition Team

There are five qualities necessary for a transition team to function in a healthy and effective way. These five qualities have been

215

adapted from Patrick Lencioni's work in *The Five Dysfunctions of a Team* and *The Advantage*. The five qualities are:

1. Team members trust each other and are genuinely vulnerable with one another.

The type of trust described here is more than the kind that says, "I trust you to tell me the truth." It is the willingness to be authentic with each other. This is part of the maturity Paul talks about in Ephesians 4:

> "Few delights can equal the presence of one whom we trust utterly."
> — George E. MacDonald

> God wants us to grow up, to know the whole truth and tell it in love — like Christ in everything. We take our lead from Christ, who is the source of everything we do. He keeps us in step with each other. His very breath and blood flow through us, nourishing us so that we will grow up healthy in God, robust in love. (Ephesians 4:15-16 TM)

Author Stephen M. R. Covey says: "The process of building trust is an interesting one, but it begins with yourself, with what I call self trust, and with your own credibility, your own trustworthiness. If you think about it, it's hard to establish trust with others if you can't trust yourself."[57]

2. Team members regularly engage in productive conflict around important issues.

We've all seen destructive conflict. It happens when the debate gets personal and relationships get hurt. Destructive conflict keeps teams from working together. At best it keeps them stuck in neutral, and at worst it moves them backwards.

> "Conflict is inevitable, but combat is optional."
> — Max Lucado

Productive conflict occurs when teams participate in passionate dialogue, disagreement, and debate in an atmosphere of mutual trust and respect. Productive conflict produces better ideas. Solomon's wisdom applies here: "Wounds from a friend can be trusted, but an enemy multiplies kisses." (Proverbs 27:6 NIV)

3. Team members leave meetings with unified agreement on next steps and a clear plan of action.

Trust and productive conflict produce good decisions, clear agreements, and a shared commitment to the next steps. That shared commitment increases the likelihood that the agreed-upon actions will in fact be carried out. C.O. Jackson said, "Great ideas need landing gears as well as wings."

> "Put God in charge of your work, then what you've planned will take place." (Proverbs 16:3 TM)

Actions are the landing gears that allow plans to arrive in reality. Friedrich Engels noted, "An ounce of action is worth a ton of theory."

4. Team members hold each another accountable to the commitments and behaviors they agreed to.

Team members who trust each other will ask each other how well they are doing on fulfilling their responsibilities. In a healthy, highly functioning team, accountability is not harsh or draining but life-giving and supportive.

> "Listen to advice and accept discipline, and at the end you will be counted among the wise." (Proverbs 19:20 NIV)

Giving an account of how they are doing is normal behavior for those who want to do their best. Leadership expert Bob Buford says, "Everyone needs a bottom line of some sort; everyone needs to be responsible, accountable to whomever it is they are serving."

5. Team members are focused on the results, not just their own agenda or individual pet project.

Effective teams push past the tendency to focus only on getting along. They engage in the demanding work of authenticity, productive conflict, shared commitment, and accountability for a reason—to accomplish results! For those working with congregations in transition, the higher purpose is the mission of Jesus.

Reflective Questions

❖ What characteristics have you seen in highly functioning, healthy teams?

❖ What are some signs of team dysfunction? How do you deal with them?

❖ What unique characteristics would a transition team have compared to other teams in congregational ministry?

Chapter 22

Blueprint Planning

T he transitional blueprint is a map designed to help the transition team, the congregational leaders, and the congregation navigate the transition. It is a fluid document that undergoes occasional reviewing and updating as new information comes to light.

The transitional blueprint is usually written by the transition team in consultation with the transitional leader, the leadership community, the congregation, and other outside leaders who are helping with the process. This chapter gives some guidance for both the development and the implementation of the transitional blueprint.

Symptoms of Not Having a Planning Blueprint

Taking the time to prayerfully and thoughtfully develop a detailed blueprint will pay off. If there is no agreement on how to proceed through the transition, some of the following symptoms will become evident:
- "drifting" from day to day
- a firefighting mentality
- leaders *reacting* rather than *responding* to situations
- lack of leadership training and development
- team and staff frustration and tension due to unclear expectations and undefined ways of working together
- low involvement from the congregation in giving and participating

The Blueprint Planning Checklist

There are a number of elements that help make the blueprint planning process a success. These elements interrelate and overlap at times. The congregational culture and context also impact the nature of the planning process.

If the congregational culture is rigid, planning will be tightly controlled. If the culture values creativity and innovation, planning will have greater flexibility. If the planning team is mature and highly functional, the planning will proceed with greater ease. If, on the other hand, the planning team is inexperienced and dysfunctional, the process will be more challenging.

> "Action without study is fatal. Study without action is futile."
> — Mary Beard

The following checklist includes a number of "to do" items intended to make the blueprint development process easier. It is written with two assumptions: 1) the eight transitional goals will be part of the conversation; and 2) a transition team is in place with the authority and responsibility to carry the plan through to completion.

Blueprint development is not done in a vacuum but is a collaborative activity. When the right people are involved in the conversations and planning process, maximum ownership and engagement will become a reality.

The blueprint planning process checklist includes the following:

1. Determine the short-term transitional vision.

As the planning journey begins, it's important to "begin with the end in mind." This means determining where "there" is. The focus at this point is not the long-term overall vision for the congregation but the vision for the transition. The questions to answer when determining where "there" should be are: What vision are we pursuing throughout this transition? What will our congregation need to look like when this transitional process is complete?

Here's an example of a short-term transitional vision (a "there"): "Our vision for this transition is to experience healing from the past, hope for the future, and the learning and renewal required to be emotionally, spiritually, relationally, and organizationally ready for our next pastor."

2. Take stock of internal and external influencing factors.

Before embarking on the journey to "there," it is helpful to know where "here" is, which is the starting point for the journey. This includes taking stock of the internal and external factors that influence where "here" is and that will have an effect on the journey to "there."

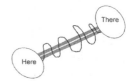

Figure 15: The Here to There Journey

These influencing factors include factors within the congregation (power brokers, history, unresolved issues, the type of transition, growth patterns, leadership strength, condition of the church building); factors within the community at large (demographics, economic climate, ethnic mix, reputation of the congregation); and factors within the denomination (theological framework, procedures and policies, available resources). Taking stock raises issues, highlights concerns, and brings to the table key information that should feed into blueprint planning.

3. Conduct an assessment of the current reality.

Assessment goes hand in hand with the survey of influencing factors. It's an ongoing process, not just a one-time event. In the beginning, assessment shows where "here" is, but later on it helps to evaluate progress toward "there."

Various assessment methods and tools are available; several are discussed at various places throughout this book. The key is to think through the goal of the assessment and what questions need to be answered in order to achieve that goal.

Here are a few of the assessment options that can be helpful in designing the transitional blueprint:

- **Interviews**

Interviews can be conducted with the congregation, the staff, the congregational leadership, and those outside the church (members who have left, former pastors, denominational leaders).

- **Surveys**

Surveys can be helpful to gather information, but some congregations have "survey fatigue." This is created by too many surveys combined with insufficient follow-through. If this is the case, it might be necessary to find another way to gather data or to first build a case for "why we should do another survey now."

- **Listening forums**

Listening forums are useful to stimulate group talking and listening. They begin with a series of questions to help people reflect and speak about key aspects of congregational life and ministry.

- **Church documents**

These include items such as vision statements, ministry plans, board minutes, staff notes, and old bulletins. Careful study of these documents will produce a deeper understanding of cultural norms, practices, and behaviors.

- **Wandering around**

This is a reminder that a lot can be learned by simply walking around. What does a tour of the church building reveal? What can be seen on Sunday morning? What's the feel of church meetings? What can be seen on the streets and sidewalks surrounding the church? How are people dressed? How loud is the music? What is the economic climate of the community?

4. Establish the main transitional goals.

The transitional vision needs a number of transitional goals written in language people understand. These are not the congregation's ultimate goals but small milestones on the way from "here" to "there." The gap is too wide to go from "here" to "there" without taking small, more achievable steps, and transitional goals will help the congregation know where it's going. Yogi Berra said, "If you don't know where you're going, you'll probably end up someplace else."

Transitional goals are the transitional team's best guess at where God is leading the congregation in the near future. They flow out of assessment and analysis and are best designed as something to "move through." In other words, the transitional team should set "goals through the goals" and remember to review and renew the goals occasionally so the congregation doesn't get stalled after one goal is achieved.

How are goals written? A proven method is to use the present tense and use words that encourage positive emotions. In addition, they should be stated as S.M.A.R.T. goals: Specific, Measureable, Achievable, Resource-able, and Time sensitive (see the textbox for more details).

> **S.M.A.R.T. Goals with a Key Question for Each**
>
> Specific — What exactly do we want to achieve?
> Measurable — How will we measure goal achievement?
> Achievable — Are we being realistic or dreaming?
> Resource-able — Do we have the resources to achieve this goal (people, money, know-how)?
> Time sensitive — When on the calendar will this be done?

5. Determine action steps to turn goals into reality.

Action steps are the landing gear for the goals. They are the tangible and measurable activities needed to reach a goal. Planning without action is useless.

> "In preparing for battle I have always found that plans are useless, but planning is indispensable."
> — Dwight D. Eisenhower

An effective planning equation looks like this: planning + action = traction. Bobb Biehl describes the interplay between planning and action this way:

> A lot of people come up with a beautiful plan. They have a detailed track laid out for the next 10 years, but take no action. Others *do* a lot, but have no clear plan. When you

combine a clear plan with action, you get traction. You begin moving from where you are to where you want to go.[58]

6. Connect action steps with people and timelines.

Any plan needs responsible, resourceful people or teams to do the work. Part of blueprint planning is working out the details of who will do what by when.

The people who do the work can come from the transition team, the leadership community, the congregation, or outside the congregation. When involving people in ministry, it is important to make sure they have the ability, support, equipping, and resources

> "The player who puts the ball through the hoop has ten hands."
> — John Wooden

to do their work. They should also have a way to report progress to those guiding their work.

7. Write and communicate the plan.

The details of the blueprint need to be written down and shared with the appropriate people. The format of each document will depend on the people it is written for. An update of the plan for the congregation will be broader in scope, while the board may need to see a detailed plan to ensure the various details are being looked after. Written communication, thoughtfully and prayerfully prepared, increases hope, lowers anxiety, and provides clear direction to everyone involved. A clearly communicated plan allows issues to be addressed, milestones to be celebrated, and the next steps to be taken.

8. Review and adjust as necessary.

It is unrealistic (and unwise) to expect to have a complete transitional blueprint at the beginning of the process. This is because the information gleaned in the early stages will inform the direction to be taken later on. This underlines the value of seeing assessment as an ongoing practice.

The frequency of reviewing and adjusting the plan depends on the complexity of the situation and the variables encountered along the way. The transitional leader, transition team, and congregational leadership need to be flexible, open to new discoveries and new direction from the Holy Spirit.

9. Acknowledge completion and celebrate success.

When the transitional process is over, it is important to celebrate. But not all celebrations should be put off until the end. It is important to take time to celebrate reaching small milestones throughout the transition. Celebration, both at the end and during the journey, helps to build momentum for change and keep people engaged.

Acknowledging the hard work and dedication of those who "made it work" will encourage further hard work. Celebrating small achievements is also an opportunity to give praise to God for his faithfulness and help throughout the process. In addition, celebrating progress fosters a positive feeling towards planning and intentional change. One of the opportunities embedded in the intentional interim model is that it teaches a congregation the value of making change a normal part of its ongoing culture. Learning how to change develops a skill a congregation will be able to use when change is needed in other areas of congregational life and ministry after the pastoral transition.

Tools for Blueprint Preparation

There are a wide variety of tools that can be used to develop the transitional blueprint. The key is to find the tool that is appropriate for the congregation's particular culture and context. The following ideas are presented as examples and as an encouragement for congregations to use research and creativity when doing planning.

Tool 1: Mind Mapping

A mind map is a way to visually present and think through the details of a plan. It can be drawn electronically, on paper, or on a white board. Here is a more complete definition:

A *mind map* is a diagram used to visually outline information. A mind map is often created around a single word or text, placed in the center, to which associated ideas, words and concepts are added. Major categories radiate from a central node, and lesser categories are sub-branches of larger branches. Categories can represent words, ideas, tasks, or other items related to a central key word or idea.[59]

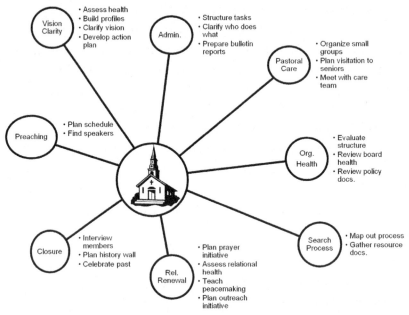

Figure 16: Mind Map of the Transitional Process

When designing a transitional plan, it is best to begin in the middle with the transitional vision and work out from there. The smaller circles are the various goal areas, with the bullet points being the action steps required to accomplish the goals. Names and dates can also be included beside each item.

Mind mapping software is available online for free or for purchase and is relatively easy to use. Two free versions to check out are Freemind and Mindjet.[60] The example presented here was created in Microsoft SmartArt, which is another option for those using Word or PowerPoint.

Tool 2: Post-it Note Planning

This is a dynamic planning process using various sized post-it notes placed on paper or a large wall. The process is useful for brainstorming as well as organizing ideas into an ordered sequence. Post-it note planning is a fluid process, allowing items to be moved around and adjusted as necessary.

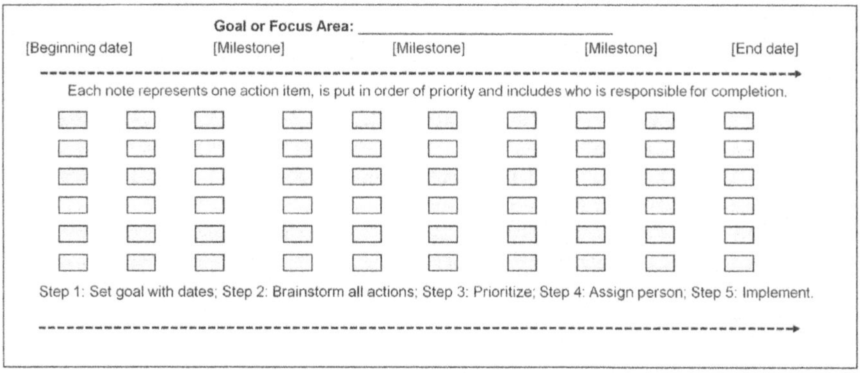

Figure 17: Post-it Note Planning Process

Post-it note planning can be done with a large group using large, letter-sized post-it notes. It can also be done at a restaurant table with small, pocket-sized post-it notes and a sheet of paper as the background.

The process consists of the following steps (based on the assumption that clearly identified goals and milestones are already in place):

Step 1: Identify all necessary actions to reach each goal and write them on post-it notes.

Step 2: Place the post-it notes on the wall or paper and organize them into groups based on the goal area they relate to.

Step 3: Prioritize the action items from most important to least important.

Step 4: Organize the action items in a time sequence matching the milestones across the top of the chart.

Step 5: Identify the person responsible for each action item.

Step 6: Agree on next steps and start implementation.

Step 7: Review progress, adjust as necessary, and re-engage until the project or plan is complete.

Tool 3: Planning Worksheet

A planning worksheet provides a structure for writing out goals, sub-goals, and action steps. Built into the planning worksheet is a place to put the names of those responsible, along with a deadline for when the task needs to be completed.

Planning Worksheet		
Goal:		
Sub-goal #1:		
Action Step	By Who?	By When?
1.		
2.		
3.		
Sub-goal #2:		
Action Step	By Who?	By When?
1.		
2.		
3.		

Figure 18: Planning Worksheet Template

Final Thoughts

Planning works best when people work the plan but remain flexible and focused throughout. Planning helps those involved to know what to say yes to and what to say no to. "The whole point of getting things done is knowing what to leave undone." (Oswald Chambers)

A blueprint for the transitional process guides decision making, gives focus to teamwork, improves morale, and helps fulfill God's purpose for his church. In the words of master planning guru Bobb Biehl, "Plans should always remain 'in pencil' (or word processing). In your mind see plans as erasable, changeable, or adaptable to tomorrow's realities."[61]

Finally, followers of Jesus should soak their planning in prayer, be informed by God's Word, and be guided by God's Spirit. The wisdom of Solomon is still true today: "In his heart a man plans his course, but the Lord determines his steps." (Proverbs 16:9 NIV) James adds: "If any of you lacks wisdom, you should ask God, who gives generously to all without finding fault, and it will be given to you." (James 1:5 NIV)

Reflective Questions

❖ What is the relationship between the process, the relationships, and the task when developing and implementing the blueprint?

❖ What planning tools will you use to facilitate your planning?

❖ How would you adjust the blueprint planning process to fit your context?

Chapter 23

Leading Change

C hange is like a multi-faceted diamond. It has many sides, yet has incredible value when handled properly. Not all change shines brightly or brings positive growth, but without change there is no growth.

> "When you're through changing, you're through."
> — Bruce Barton

A congregation in transition is made up of people thrust into a change they may or may not have wished for. On the surface, the congregation is being asked to say goodbye to its pastor, let go of the past, and prepare to move on and follow a new leader. Under the surface, it may be experiencing strong emotions, developing fierce resistance to change, and wrestling with many unanswered questions.

Unless the transitional process is led well, long-term problems can persist. If there is a good understanding of how change and transition work, there is a good possibility that the congregation will be well prepared for the next season of its ministry life.

> "If nothing changes, nothing changes."
> — Unknown

The Two Kinds of Change

Two basic types of change are technical change and adaptive change. Technical change is required in a situation where a problem is solvable with the skills, know-how, and resources currently available. Adaptive change is appropriate when the needed change requires new thinking, a different perspective, and some experimentation.

An example of technical change is changing a flat tire on a car. The driver has probably changed a tire before and has the necessary know-how, resources, and experience. It will not take any creativity or deep thinking to accomplish the change.

An example of adaptive change is when a salesman comes to the door and says, "I'd like you to consider buying these new tires that require no air and never go flat." To make this change requires new thinking, a different perspective, and a good enough reason to spend a rather large sum of money for the new technology. The change seems unnecessary, so in order for a switch to be made, the barriers to switching must be removed.

A congregation in transition experiences both technical and adaptive change. When the problem is solvable with the skill set, procedures, and know-how already existing in the congregation, it's relatively easy and technical in nature.

If the change required is adaptive in nature, new skills must be learned, a new perspective achieved, experimentation practiced, and adjustments made. Adaptive change must reach the emotional and intellectual level to be effective. For the intentional interim to be transformational, adaptive change will have to be part of the equation.

A Deeper Look at the Change Process

This chapter is based on an assumption: Change is not just an event, but a process. This process must be looked at from a variety of perspectives to develop an understanding of how it works and how it can be led. Leaders can't lead what they don't understand.

The change process can be better understood by looking at it from three perspectives: the change journey, the eight stages of organizational change, and the three elements people need to make a change. Each of these perspectives will show how change is both something traveled through as well as something people need help with. The change process consists of events, stages, and experiences. Knowing what to expect during a season of change equips transitional leaders to guide both themselves and others through the ups and downs and ins and outs of change.

The time between pastors is fertile ground for positive change to occur, but it takes wise leadership to navigate the turbulence often found there. Leadership expert Peter Drucker says:

One cannot manage change. One can only be ahead of it. In a period of upheavals, such as the one we are living in, change is the norm. To be sure, it is painful and risky, and above all it requires a great deal of very hard work. But unless it is seen as the task of the organization to lead change, the organization will not survive. In a period of rapid structural change, the only ones who survive are the change leaders. A change leader sees change as an opportunity. A change leader looks for change, knows how to find the right changes, and knows how to make them effective both outside the organization and inside it.[62]

The Change Journey

Change can be represented visually as a change journey. This is one key perspective to view change from.

In the change journey diagram, the horizontal axis represents the passage of time. The vertical axis represents ability, competence, and confidence. During the change journey, ability, competence, and confidence drop off. Eventually, abilities will increase again after new learning and positive progress have been achieved.

The *present mountain* (1) is where the congregation begins the change journey and the place the congregation must eventually leave behind. It's the sum total of all the

> "Change before you have to."
> — Jack Welch

investments made to date. It's the place of comfort and security. It isn't necessarily a bad place, but it must be given up in exchange for something different and better. The role of the change agent is to help people identify if their *present mountain* is an obstacle or a motivator to the changes they need to make.

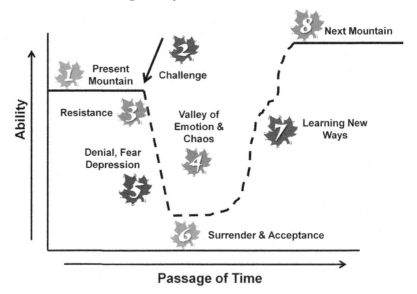

Figure 19: The Change Journey

The *challenge* (2) is the event or person initiating the change, not the change itself. The *challenge* threatens the *present mountain* and comes from inside or outside the congregation. The key is to help people feel they have some control over the changes being made. Giving control includes giving people as much information as possible, so that they gain clarity about why a *next mountain* (8) is needed.

Resistance (3) is closely related to *denial, fear, and depression* (5). They are part of the *valley of emotion and chaos* (4). Sometimes emotions are perceived as obstacles to change, but in reality they are a natural part of the change journey and something to work through. It should not be surprising when people resist change after they have made such a huge investment in the current structure.

People who resist change are often asking "Why should I throw away my hard earned *present mountain*?" They aren't always trying to be difficult. The wise coach and change agent allows questions to be asked, provides information to help people with their concerns, and practices the "ministry of presence" with those who struggle. Time spent with resisters may be time well spent because they could become positive supporters.

Chaos (4) is what happens when a *challenge* comes along, disturbs the *present mountain,* and invites those heavily invested in the *present mountain* to be thrown into the *valley of emotion* (4). Out of *chaos,* new opportunity emerges. Eventually, *surrender and acceptance* (6) pave the way for new opportunities and growth towards a new beginning.

Learning new ways (7) follows *surrender and acceptance* and emerges as the congregation grows comfortable with a new way of doing things. There may be moments of grief as members remember the past and feel they'd rather be back at the *present mountain.* But when healthy change is happening, the climb involves new learning, growth, and embracing what lies ahead.

The *next mountain* (8) is the place where new competencies and new behaviors become comfortable. It feels good to be there. For the congregation in transition, there emerges an excitement for a new beginning and a readiness to embrace the new season. The new season, however, needs to be held with an open hand since the *next mountain* becomes the new *present mountain.*

Eight Stages of Organizational Change

A second perspective to look from when thinking about change is to look at the various stages or actions required to lead a change. The core challenge in leading change is shifting people's behavior.

John Kotter describes how it's done: "Changing behavior is less a matter of giving people analysis to influence their thoughts than helping them to see a truth to influence their feelings. Both thinking and feeling are essential, and both are found in successful organizations, but the heart of change is in the emotions."[63]

Stage or Action	New Behavior	Comments
Increase urgency for change.	People start telling each other, "Let's go. We need to change things!"	Focus on developing a sense of urgency among "the key influencers." The critical mass must be sufficient to overcome complacency, fear, or anger (all of which undermine change).
Build a guiding team.	A group strong enough to guide the change comes together and starts working.	Pull together the credibility, skills, connections, reputations, and formal authority required to provide change leadership. Work together. Discourage the lone ranger. Build trust.
Develop a change vision.	The guiding team develops the right vision and strategy for the change effort.	Create a sensible, clear, simple, uplifting vision with a strategy. Take a risk, and don't get bogged down in details just yet.
Communicate for ownership.	People begin to buy into the change, and this shows in their behavior.	Send simple heartfelt messages through multiple channels to promote understanding, develop gut-level commitment, and free up more energy from more people. Deeds surpass words. Use symbols. Repeat often!
Empower action by removing barriers.	More people feel able to act, and do act on the vision.	Remove any roadblocks or barriers to change (processes or people). Don't leave your people to fend for themselves—be available to remove any obstacles in the way of the change.
Create short-term wins.	Momentum builds as people try to fulfill the vision—and fewer and fewer resist change.	Help people achieve short-term wins—they fuel the overall change. Manage the process carefully so the right projects are selected, the ones the critics and cynics can't sabotage.
Maintain momentum.	Make wave after wave of changes until the vision is fulfilled. Don't give up!	Momentum builds after the early wins. But don't try to do too much at once. Build slowly and intentionally. Seek feedback. Listen constantly.
Make change stick.	New and winning behaviors continue despite the pull of the past.	Making change stick means nurturing a new culture. Clarify the new behaviors to be repeated and notice shared values. Key events matter.

Table 4: Eight Stages of Organizational Change

Factors People Need to Make a Change

A third perspective to view change from is to look at the elements required for people to make a change. These ideas are an adaptation of the work of Chip and Dan Heath in their book *Switch: How to Make Change When Change is Hard.*

For people to change, they need three things. First, they need *direction.* This speaks to the rational side of change. Second, they need *motivation.* This speaks to the emotional side of change. The energy and motivation needed for change come from emotion. Third, people need *simplification* if they are going to make a change. The change must be made easy, which includes providing a simple pathway for people to follow during the change process.

Chip and Dan Heath use a change metaphor involving a rider and an elephant. The emotional side of change is represented by the elephant while the rational side is represented by the rider. Both sides need to work together:

> If you want to change things, you've got to appeal to both. The Rider provides the planning and direction, and the Elephant provides the energy. So if you reach the Riders of your team but not the Elephants, team members will have understanding without motivation. If you reach the Elephants but not their Riders, they'll have passion without direction. In both cases, the flaws can be paralyzing. A reluctant Elephant and a wheel-spinning Rider can both ensure that nothing changes. But when Elephants and Riders move together, change can come easily.[64]

The following is a deeper look at the three elements necessary to make change easier. They are presented as coming from the mouth of a leader engaged in leading change.

1. To make a change, people need to be given direction.

- *You give direction by spotting people doing things right and then having other people imitate them.*

Example: "Thanks, John, for picking up the chairs without being asked. I'd encourage those watching to follow John's example and find ways to serve and be helpful without being asked."

- *You give direction by describing the exact behavior you want people to embrace.*

Example: "These talking guidelines we've put on the whiteboard are there to guide us in the way we will interact with each other tonight. Do we all agree to follow them?"

- *You give direction by showing people the destination, then telling them why it's important to go there.*

Example: "By the time we begin the search process, we want to have a board of elders who trust each other, practice productive conflict, make commitments, and are accountable for what they have said they would do. This is important because it's a practical way to obey Jesus' command to love one another and work as one."

2. To make a change, people need a boost in motivation.

- *You boost motivation by connecting people with a positive feeling.*

Example: "When thinking of a change in our Sunday service musical style, I want you to consider what it would feel like if you had your grandchildren sitting with you in church, listening to music they could resonate with and enjoy."

- *You boost motivation by reducing fear, which is done by breaking change down into bite-sized pieces.*

Example: "We're looking for small group leaders. As a small group leader, all you need to do is insert a DVD and when it's finished, ask these five questions."

- *You boost motivation by giving people an identity to embrace.*

Example: "Imagine what it would be like for our church to be known as the church that does random acts of kindness in our neighborhood. Working backwards from that image of ourselves, what can we do to make it a reality?"

3. To make a change, people need someone to bring simplification.

- *You bring simplification by modifying the environment so people will act differently.*

Example: "We are going to start having board meetings at Fred's house. Fred's wife Alice is an amazing cook and has offered to make supper for us before every meeting."

- *You bring simplification by helping people form new habits to make the changes automatic.*

Example: "We are going to take the entire congregation through '40 Days of Purpose' to help form the habit of small group attendance and promote spiritual growth in our people."

- *You bring simplification by using peer pressure to shape behavior.*

Example: "George, if you keep being disrespectful of others in meetings, how will your sister-in-law Mary feel about your behavior? She's sitting right here!"

Reflective Questions

- ❖ Think of a significant change you made this past year. Describe how you felt and what you did to achieve the change and handle the feelings.

- ❖ Give an example of technical change and an example of adaptive change.

- ❖ Reflect on the eight stages of organizational change. What stage do you find most challenging and why?

Leading Effective Change When Change Was Hard

The Church on the Prairie had been struggling for many years, largely because of a very domineering member, one who might be called a bully. Whether he was on the board or not, he badgered members with phone calls until they followed his wishes. He was responsible for getting pastors fired and blocking the hiring of good pastoral candidates he did not personally like. This destructive behavior went on for 16 years, according to one member.

When the church was looking for another pastor, the district coach told the board chairman, "We don't want to see you put up with this behavior any longer. If you agree to it, I and the denomination will commit to working with you to help you become a healthy church."

The district coach then listed six conditions and commitments as the pathway for going forward. Two of the most challenging conditions were to suspend the congregation's autonomy for one year and, under the leadership of the coach, to ask the bully to leave. The latter recommendation came after careful research, both inside and outside the church. The board accepted all six recommendations.

The church worked through the issues prayerfully and carefully. As emotions subsided, plans were made to begin the search for a new pastor. The Lord had just the right person in mind. After he arrived, the new pastor spent most of his time the first year developing the congregational leaders, who responded with commitment and enthusiasm. Within three years, the church grew to a healthy 100 people, with baptisms almost every month. After six years, the congregation remodeled and expanded the church building in order to accommodate the growing congregation. The church continued to grow and enjoy the ministry of an effective staff, with attendance growing to over 300 people.

– Abe Funk

Chapter 24

Managing Conflict

W hen conflict surfaces during the time between pastors, a Christian vision is needed for managing that conflict. It's not a matter of *if* people disagree but *when*. It is inevitable. What's not inevitable is how people respond to the disagreement.

One authority on managing conflict says:

How Christians behave in conflict is of critical moral and spiritual consequence...As John observed, "Whoever says, 'I am in the light,' while hating his brother or sister, is still in the darkness" (1 John 2:9)...What is a Christian vision for managing conflicts? A Christian vision of shalom...a wholeness that incorporates God's reconciling love, justice, redemption, liberation, truthfulness, and compassion... God's peace provides the ultimate Christian vision for what makes a church fight Christian.[65]

Unresolved or mismanaged conflict interrupts relationship renewal. If the goal of the transitional process is to prepare the congregation for a healthy re-engagement with its next senior pastor, then the time

> The time between senior pastors is an opportunity for assessing and addressing unresolved and mismanaged conflict.

between pastors is an opportunity for assessing and addressing unresolved and mismanaged conflict. If left unresolved or mismanaged, the conflict will continue to interrupt peace in the community of faith.

This chapter addresses several factors that escalate or de-escalate negative conflict. It provides a working definition of conflict, a review of two approaches to dealing with conflict, and a description of five conflict styles. It also offers some guidance on how to assess congregational conflict. The goal is to encourage a deeper pursuit of biblical peacemaking.

Factors Affecting Negative Conflict in the Church

Like most family systems, congregations are often to some extent dysfunctional in the way they deal with differences and conflict. What makes matters worse is that churches are often unaware of how they handle conflict, have a tendency to avoid dealing with conflict, and have leaders with little training in conflict management.

Here are some common factors in churches' handling of conflict:

- Churches avoid dealing directly and quickly with interpersonal conflict when it arises and allow it to fester towards damaging levels.
- Churches spend inadequate time assessing the nature and context of conflict to determine how to adequately respond to it biblically.
- Churches react with inappropriate and immature responses to conflict because they are not comfortable with conflict.
- Churches misapply Matthew 18 in order to remove the people who make them uncomfortable without clearly identifying what sin was committed (if any).
- Churches treat vocal minorities or immature voices harshly when they attempt to speak up about an issue, especially if it involves leadership.
- Churches miss opportunities to listen to those who might have something valuable to say because they overreact to the awkward or hurtful ways those people speak.
- People in churches do not look at their own role in conflict by asking questions such as: How does this

conflict affect me? What about this conflict is my doing? Why am I in this conflict?

Conflict Escalation and De-escalation

Conflict escalates when certain conditions are present and de-escalates when other conditions exist. Knowing this will help reduce the damaging effects of negative conflict.

> "Difficulties are meant to rouse, not discourage. The human spirit is to grow strong by conflict." — William E. Channing

Conflict escalates when the following conditions exist:

- Bystanders become involved and take sides.
- One party (or both parties) feels threatened by the other.
- There is no interest or investment in maintaining the relationship.
- There is an increase in the acting out of anger, fear, and frustration.
- Important needs are not acknowledged or met.

Conflict de-escalates when the following conditions exist:

- Those involved focus on the problem instead of each other.
- Emotions of anger, fear, and frustration are expressed directly rather than demonstrated indirectly.
- Real and perceived threats are eliminated or at least addressed.
- Needs are openly discussed and acknowledged.

Defining Conflict

Conflict is like a rubber band. When there is too little tension, the rubber band won't function. When there is too much tension, the rubber band becomes dangerous. Too much tension in relationships has negative consequences. Too little tension makes those relationships unproductive.

One way to move towards an understanding of what "proper tension" looks like is to provide some definitions of conflict. Far too often, people see conflict as negative, but, by definition, conflict is more neutral than negative. It is how people behave in conflict that makes it constructive or destructive. The benefit of defining conflict is that it creates the needed space to talk about the value of conflict for personal and congregational growth.

Ken Sande defines conflict as "a difference of opinion or purpose that frustrates someone's purpose or desire. It may range from good natured differences to minor frictions, to aggressive confrontations."[66]

Ressler Schrock-Shenk says, "Conflict is a disagreement between interdependent people;

> Conflict = differences + tension
> — Ressler Schrock-Shenk

it is the perception of incompatible or mutually exclusive needs or goals. Put more simply, conflict equals differences plus tension."[67]

The Justice Institute of British Columbia defines conflict as "differences between at least two interdependent parties who perceive or are experiencing: incompatible goals or needs, different processes/routes to a goal, interference in meeting their goals or needs."[68]

Conflict Myths

Family systems, including church family systems, often have "rules" or "myths" about conflict that determine how it is handled, including whether conflict is addressed openly or avoided. A transitional leader should listen carefully for the rules defining the culture of conflict in the congregation. While listening, the leader will be able to discern how, when, and if he or she should address the conflict. For instance, listening will help the leader know whether to address conflict directly (through intervention) or indirectly (through preaching and other non-direct means).

Here are a few of the myths that may exist in a congregation that can keep it from effectively utilizing conflict for growth:

- If conflict is present, that is a sign of bad leadership.
- Conflict must be bad because it threatens our unity.
- Conflict is a sign of ungodly relationships or ungodly people.
- Being *spiritual* is defined as "being above and without conflict."
- Conflict is actually sin, so we had better get rid of it.
- We'll be better as soon as we resolve the conflict and move on!
- Jesus didn't have conflict, so we shouldn't either.
- If we disagree, someone is not hearing from God or believing the right things.
- A loving and godly person is always tranquil, stable, and serene and never experiences conflict.

How to address these myths will be dealt with later in this chapter. However, first, it will be helpful to look at the leader in conflict and provide some help for self-monitoring and self-assessment in conflict.

Self-assessment in Conflict

A trained transitional leader increases a congregation's capacity to value the redemptive and therapeutic aspects of conflict. The transitional leader has the opportunity to address past mismanaged conflict and prepare for future conflicts by introducing new thinking and behavior.

> Who we are in conflict directly affects what we bring to a congregation in conflict.

A healthy and holy approach to conflict begins by understanding the dynamics of congregational conflict and ends with modeling biblical conflict management and peacemaking. However, before dealing with the congregation's approach to conflict, the transitional leader must first assess his or her own approach to conflict. In order to conduct a self-assessment, the transitional leader needs to ask: "Who am I in conflict?"

Transitional leaders bring their own approach to conflict into a congregation even if they are unaware of having one. How the transitional leader handles conflict directly affects what the transitional leader brings to a congregation in conflict. Resources for self-assessment are listed in Chapter 16.

Factors Influencing People in Conflict

Specific influences determine how people approach conflict and how they interpret the behavior of others in conflict. These influences include their experiences, their beliefs, and their unique genetic disposition. Two crucial influences are culture and family of origin.

- **Culture**

Culture includes ethnicity, gender, theology, age, geographical neighborhood, associations (musicians, athletes, artists), and subcultures within each association (jazz musicians, country singers, runners, football fans). Values, viewpoints, and behavioral patterns are influenced by these things and are triggered in conflict.

- **Family of Origin**

How a person's family dealt with conflict—the unspoken rules of engagement, the behaviors that were affirmed or punished— affects how they deal with conflict today. People's approaches to conflict develop over time and without much thought.

Each approach can be useful in some circumstances. However, there are other situations where a person's preferred approach gets a negative reaction or leaves the person confused about what just happened. In those situations, adjusting the approach to conflict may be helpful. Although a person's habitual style will surface more often under stress, it is possible for people to change their conflict management style through awareness.

Approaches to Conflict Management

There are two general approaches to conflict: adversarial and cooperative. The chosen approach will invoke trust and transparency (cooperative) or protection and defensiveness (adversarial). Increasing awareness about his or her own approach to conflict will increase the transitional leader's capacity to manage conflict effectively.

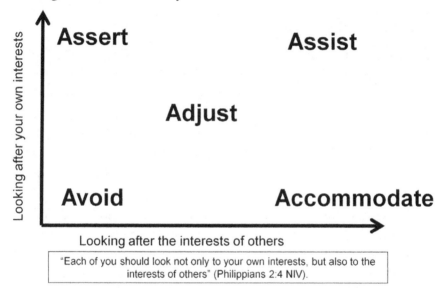

"Each of you should look not only to your own interests, but also to the interests of others" (Philippians 2:4 NIV).

Figure 20: Five Common Responses to Conflict

Most of the literature on conflict styles includes at least five common responses to conflict: avoid, accommodate, assist (collaborate), adjust (compromise), and assert (direct).

1. **Avoid** — It says, "No way!"

The avoidance style is uncooperative and non-assertive in conflict. It does not look after its own interests or the interests of others.

2. **Accommodate** — It says, "Your way!"

The accommodating style is cooperative and non-assertive. It looks after the interests of others but not its own interests.

3. **Assert** — It says, "My way!"

The assertive style is uncooperative and assertive. It looks after its own interests but not the interests of others.

4. **Adjust** — It says, "Halfway!"

The adjusting style is partly cooperative and partially assertive. It lets go of some of its own interests for some of the interests of others.

5. **Assist** — It says, "Our way!"

The assist style is fully cooperative and fully assertive. It looks after its own interests and the interests of others.

Paul's admonition in Philippians 2:4 implies that people will naturally look after their own interests: "Each of you should look not only to your own interests, but also to the interests of others." (NIV) Paul does not deny or correct this aspect of human life. He adds value to human relationships by calling us to look at (pay attention to) the interests of others without totally discarding our own interests. Looking after our own interests allows others to know what is important to us in any given situation.

We might demonstrate love for others by putting their interests first (accommodating), or we might demonstrate love for others by declaring our needs to them (asserting). Either way, we can express love and work collaboratively in all of these styles. An unhealthy pattern emerges when we always approach conflict with one predominant style that ignores either our needs or the needs of others.

Assessing and Addressing Congregational Conflict

It is critical for a transitional leader to correctly assess a situation before making recommendations for a particular course of action. There are three general areas to look at when doing an assessment: the type of conflict, the sources of the conflict, and the level of the conflict.

Below is a summary of what to look for in each of the three areas when doing an assessment.

1. The Type of Conflict

There are several perspectives to consider when assessing the type of conflict. The following words help define the various viewpoints and offer some examples of how the conflict might show up in a congregational setting:

- **Internal** — e.g., indecision, substance abuse, bitterness
- **Substantive** — e.g., whether to adopt a new curriculum or build an addition
- **Values and beliefs** — e.g., doctrine, program priorities
- **Relationships** — e.g., personal offenses, unforgiveness, divorce
- **Information** — e.g., selective release of information, misrepresentation
- **System** — e.g., confusion regarding responsibilities or chain of command

2. The Source of the Conflict

Conflict can come from a variety of sources or starting points. Discerning the sources continues to peel back the onion of conflict to see it more clearly. The following words help explain various sources of conflict:

- **Communication** — e.g., misunderstanding, lack of information, assumptions, differences in perspective, misinformation, and unclear information
- **Relationships** — e.g., stereotypes, distorted perceptions, unmet expectations, fear, and use of power
- **Structures** — e.g., ineffective processes; time constraints; inappropriate structures, organizations, social structures, and systems
- **Interests** — e.g., perceived or actual incompatibility of needs and interests; differences in preferences, styles,

and ways of doing things; differences in emotional needs
- **Values** — e.g., opposing beliefs, values, philosophies, and worldviews

3. The Levels of Conflict

Speed Leas describes several levels of conflict,[69] from the least problematic to the most damaging. The level of the conflict impacts the approach that should be taken to resolve it.
- **Level 0: Depression**

This level says, "I'm not in conflict." This is anger turned inward and indicates a lack of awareness of unhealthy conflict. Depression is the prevailing emotion and the conflict is not openly acknowledged or recognized.
- **Level 1: Problem to Solve**

This level says, "I want to work on this with you, collaborate, and find a mutually beneficial solution." There is conflict around goals, values, and needs.
- **Level 2: Disagreement**

This level says, "I want to come out looking good but still solve the problem." Personalities are starting to surface, and problems are becoming more difficult to define.
- **Level 3: Dispute or Contest**

This level says, "I want to win, and that means you will lose." Personal attacks are starting, and "sides" and "camps" are forming.
- **Level 4: Fight or Flight**

This level says, "I want to hurt you, hurt the opposition, or escape." The factions are starting to solidify, and the conversation has shifted to talking about principles, not issues.
- **Level 5: Intractable Situation**

This level says, "I will hurt you or annihilate you." The conflict is unmanageable, and the energy is centered on eliminating the opposing person.

Speed Leas suggests that conflict should be seen as an opportunity for growth, not as a weakness:

The aim of a well-managed conflict process is to help individuals become stronger rather than weaker. Conflict can be an opportunity to grow and develop; it does not have to be equated with illness, which weakens the body unless eradicated. It can be an opportunity to learn about yourself and how you manage under tension. It can be an opportunity to practice new behaviors and assess their relevance to other conflict situations (present or future) in your life. Conflict is like tennis; you can't learn how to do it by watching, you have to be in it to learn and to develop your skill. I am not suggesting that one should create conflict for the learning opportunities it affords, but I am suggesting that unless we learn from good experiences in the present, we will be likely to repeat bad experiences in the future.[70]

Benefits of Healthy and Holy Conflict Management

There are several benefits a congregation can experience if it embraces conflict and deals with it in a productive and redemptive manner. Those benefits include:

- healthier relationships once the journey through the conflict has been completed
- restoration of believers who return after pulling away
- growth in spiritual maturity, along with greater engagement in faith-building practices
- stronger families due to new conflict management behaviors that were learned with the church family now being applied at home
- leaders with increased credibility and respect because they have learned to deal clearly and carefully with conflict
- elimination and avoidance of fatal divisions that might have occurred had the conflict been allowed to escalate

- an increase in the purity and unity of the congregation
- protection of much needed resources for kingdom advancement and less exposure to unnecessary lawsuits

Pathways to Peace

When interpersonal peace is disturbed through negative conflict, making peace will require rebuilding trust, resolving issues, repairing hearts, and restoring relationships.

Figure 21: Pathways to Peace

1. Rebuilding Trust

Trust is the foundation that allows the benefits of conflict to be maximized. When trust is broken, conflict is difficult to manage, and relationships are endangered. Trust is built by learning more about the other person's situation, perspective, interests, and assumptions.

> Reconciliation is a process of the heart and mind without a guarantee about the outcome.

A transitional leader facilitates movement towards peace by helping people gain an understanding of each other's perspectives through active listening and assertive engagement. This requires stepping into the other person's shoes. It also requires practicing the principle of seeking first to understand before being understood.

A simple tool for motivating people to build trust is to hold an object (such as a cell phone) between those who see things differently and asking both to describe what they see from their perspective. The answers will be quite different, especially if the cell phone has a picture of the transitional leader's latest grandson on the screen. The leader can then ask, "Without moving the object, how can you see what the other person sees?" The answer might be to ask the person on the other side to share more about what he or she sees. Or it might be that the first person will have to move around to the other side of the object and look at what the other person sees. Most people will get the message, move off their need to be heard, and start listening to the other perspective.

When listening to someone else's perspective, it's appropriate to test assumptions about the conflict. This is done by asking open questions and staying curious. The tendency to judge another person by jumping to conclusions decreases trust. A genuine desire to seek clarification is a step towards building trust.

2. Resolving Issues

Unresolved issues are often the rubble preventing peace from being made in a relationship. There is an inclination to want to leap to an apology and forgiveness without addressing the concrete issues that initiated the conflict or broke the relationship in the first place. This rubble remains a barrier to peace if it is not acknowledged and unless the parties mutually agree on how to deal with it.

Substantive matters that need resolution might include salary, money owed, time spent together, use of space, borrowed property, or damaged materials. The matter might not be addressed fully at this stage. Sometimes simply acknowledging that there was a problem is all that's needed.

Relational matters can often be more difficult since they usually have an emotional component. If unaddressed, these relational matters have the potential of stalling peace between people.

3. Repairing Hearts

Once trust has been rebuilt and some level of satisfaction has been reached about resolving the issues, it is time to move on to heart issues. This requires acknowledging wrongdoing (sin), apologizing with specific words, asking for forgiveness, accepting forgiveness, and making amends.

"I'm sorry if I hurt you" or "I'm sorry but..." is not an apology. It is a deflection from the hard work of taking ownership for one's contribution to the conflict and hinders true peacemaking.

The components of a full apology include:

- **Acknowledgement** – clearly identifying the issue affecting the other person
- **Apology** – using the words "I am sorry" without using "if," "but," or "and"
- **Asking for forgiveness** – using the words "Will you forgive me?" along with a description of the issue
- **Accepting forgiveness** – waiting for the other person to respond in freedom and receiving the grace of forgiveness when it is offered
- **Arranging amends** – checking to see what compensation might be required and offering it to the other person

4. Restoring Relationship

Reconciliation is not guaranteed because it requires two repaired hearts. Each person is responsible for his or her part of the solution but cannot make the other person respond. A reconciled relationship restores peace between people even if their current relationship is not the same as it was before the disturbance. In other words, the two might not plan to go golfing or go for a walk together again, but they will not avoid golfing or walking for fear of running into the other person.

Ken Sande, in his book *The Peacemaker*, offers a helpful pathway for restoring relationships. He defines forgiveness as a decision to make four promises: 1) I will not dwell on this incident; 2) I will not bring up this incident again and use it against you; 3) I will not talk to others about this incident; and 4) I will not let this incident stand between us or hinder our personal relationship.[71]

The first promise is unconditional and is about letting go of the incident so the offended heart can be free to move on. The other three are conditional because they depend on the response of the other person. Making and keeping these promises tears down the walls that stand between the offender and the other person. It clears the way for the relationship to develop unhindered by memories of past wrongs. Sande observes, "This is exactly what God does for us, and it is what he calls us to do for others."[72]

Peace between people is a precious gift. When it is disturbed, the pathway to peace is hard work. The work of reconciliation is worth it if people are to honor the Lord Jesus and walk in the *agape* love of the Father.

Reflective Questions

❖ What hinders the church from dealing with conflict in a productive and Christ-honoring way?

❖ What factors have influenced your personal view of conflict?

❖ What incidents from Jesus' life correspond to the five styles of responding to conflict (avoid, accommodate, assert, adjust, and assist)?

Chapter 25

Facilitating the Model

F acilitate comes from the Latin word *facilis* and means "to make easy." A facilitator guides a process and helps participants travel from where they are to where they hope to be. Facilitation is both an art and a science. It's learned through a combination of study and practice, with greater weight put on practice and "learning-by-doing."

Facilitation is an essential competency of the transitional leader in a congregation. It is the oil that reduces the friction during the transitional process, the practical leadership that helps make the transition run a lot smoother.

Ingrid Bens, in her book *Facilitation at a Glance!*, defines the facilitator this way: "One who contributes structure and process to interactions so groups are able to function effectively and make high-quality decisions. A helper and enabler whose goal is to support others to achieve exceptional performance."[73]

The Three Legs of Facilitation

There are three aspects of healthy facilitation that work together in harmony: the process, the goal or task, and the relationships. All three aspects need to be kept in mind when working with a group to make their conversations easier. If the

Figure 22: Legs of Facilitation

task or goal is overemphasized at the expense of relationships, people may struggle emotionally, feel rushed, and check out of the process. If the process is unclear and meetings are poorly planned, valuable time is wasted and progress is stalled. If the focus is only on relationships, people may feel warm and fuzzy, but the real issues may be ignored.

Factors for Facilitation

The facilitator introduces, models, and guides the process. To create an environment where conversations are easier, the facilitator encourages positive factors and avoids negative factors.

Positive Factors to Encourage

- **Safety** — creating a place where people can be honest and open
- **Trust** — establishing a climate where transparency and being real are encouraged
- **Productive conflict** — teaching people to disagree without being disagreeable
- **Caring confrontation** — teaching people to confront one another in love and with respect
- **Open questioning** — allowing people to question ideas without fear of reprisal
- **Respect** — teaching people to value the opinions of each other without judging
- **Diversity** — allowing people to have different perspectives and continue to feel valued
- **Active listening** — helping people to seek first to understand and then to be understood
- **Learning** — encouraging the ability to learn, grow, and find solutions
- **Curiosity** — nurturing a child-like exploration of what could be

- **Clear agenda** — taking time to clarify the reason for the conversation and the group goals for the conversation

Negative Factors to Avoid

- judging or coercing people
- forcing people to change
- imposing values on others
- allowing a certain few to dominate the conversation
- exhibiting a lack of belief in people's ability to come up with answers
- avoiding failure at all costs
- moving as quickly as possible away from awkward moments
- seeing the tools as more important than the process
- failing to provide ground rules and discussion parameters
- leaving the action to be taken as a result of the conversation unclear

What Kind of Facilitation Is Best?

One way to decide what kind of facilitation to use is to consider a grid comparing problem-focused facilitation and solution-focused facilitation.[74] Problem-focused facilitation looks to solve problems by closely investigating their causes and determining what can be done to reduce their influence on the group. It looks at what's feeding the problem, why it continues to be a problem, and how persons involved can try harder to overcome the problem. The focus is to learn as much as possible about the problem in order to discover how to eliminate the problem.

Solution-focused facilitation does not ignore the problems, but works on helping people to identify, develop, and implement solutions to the problem. It centers around what the people involved want, looks for what's currently working, and encourages doing more of what is already working. This approach looks for new ways to do things rather than trying harder to use the old ways.

PROBLEM-FOCUSED Facilitation	SOLUTION-FOCUSED Facilitation
• centers on reducing the problem • looks at what participants are doing wrong • emphasizes what participants don't want • highlights what could be done better • seeks to eliminate negative weaknesses • interested in "why" the problem happens (What causes and maintains this problem?)	• centers on enhancing the solution • looks at what participants are doing right • emphasizes what participants want • highlights what is already being done well • seeks to accentuate positive strengths • interested in when the problem doesn't happen (Any exceptions to the problem?)

Table 5: Problem and Solution-focused Facilitation

Creating Ground Rules for Facilitation

Taking time to create ground rules before launching into a facilitated conversation is essential. Ground rules describe the way a group should interact and create a safe, even playing field.

One effective way to create ground rules is for the facilitator to take five to ten minutes at the beginning of the session to write on a white board or sheet of paper the rules for the group's interaction. The facilitator should then remove any rules the group feels are unnecessary and add any rules the group feels are missing. The key is to make sure everyone agrees to the rules before beginning the conversation.

Some common ground rules to include are:
- Start and end on time.
- Speak respectfully to each other.

- Practice active listening with each other.
- Practice confidentiality (what is discussed in the room stays in the room).
- Respect each other's experiences, differences, and perspectives.
- Come prepared for each meeting or conversation.
- Stay focused while present and eliminate distractions (turn off phones, commit to staying for the whole time).
- Encourage everyone to speak.
- Have everyone agree to participate fully during the meeting.

Facilitation and Asking Questions

The ability to ask powerful questions in a timely fashion is a critical skill for effective facilitation. Questions assist in gathering information and open the door to dialogue and discovery. An experienced facilitator keeps a collection of questions readily available to be used when needed. A good question travels well and can be used repeatedly.

Following are a few questions that can be used at various times during the transitional process. They are presented in various categories to make using them easier. The questions are written as if the facilitator were to ask them. The recipient of the questions could be the congregation, the transition team, or the church leadership.

Setting up the Transitional Process

- What's the history and background of this congregation?
- What are the expectations of the transitional leader, the church leadership, and the congregation during the transitional process?

- Who will be responsible to give leadership to the eight goal areas of the transitional process?
- What tools will we use in the assessment process?
- Who will serve on the transition team, and how will the members be chosen?
- What role will the denomination play in the transition?
- How would you describe the health and capacity of the board and leadership community?
- What is the level of congregational ownership for the transitional process? How would you describe the congregation's readiness for change?
- What type of exit did the previous pastor have?
- Is there any unfinished business we need to attend to?

Preaching

- How will the preaching direction be established?
- Who will preach? How will the preaching schedule be facilitated?
- How is communication flowing between the leadership and the congregation?
- How will the progress of the transition be communicated to the congregation?

Pastoral Care

- How will we organize pastoral care during the transition?
- What will the role of the transitional leader be in pastoral care?
- What needs adjusting in order for us to provide adequate pastoral care?

Administration

- How will we handle the oversight of the day-to-day ministry?

- What administrative role will the transitional leader have?
- What are the gaps in the way regular ministry is organized?

Closure

- What type of transition are we dealing with (smooth, rough, crisis)? What factors lead to that conclusion?
- What role will the church leadership, the congregation, and the transitional leader play in bringing closure to the past?
- What activities, meetings, processes, or conversations will we use to help facilitate healthy closure from the past?

Relationship Renewal

Upward

- On a scale of 1-10 (10 being strong and 1 being weak), how would you rate the overall health of this congregation in terms of the quality of the members' relationship with God? What do you base your answer on?
- What do we need to do to foster increased health and vitality in our relationship with God?

Inward

- On a scale of 1-10 (10 being strong and 1 being weak), how would you rate the overall relational health between people in this congregation? What do you base your answer on?
- What would growth in relational health look like?
- Are there any unresolved conflicts in this congregation needing attention? If yes, what process will we use to deal with them?

Outward

- On a scale of 1-10 (10 being strong and 1 being weak), how would you rate the outward relationship engagement of this congregation with those not yet following Jesus? What would greater engagement look like?
- What could we do during our transition to increase outward impact?

Vision Clarity

- Why does this congregation exist?
- What does this congregation stand for?
- What will the future look like if things go as planned?
- What activities will be core to this congregation's life and ministry?
- What is the strategy or plan for ministry success?
- What are the most important priorities we need to focus on right now?
- Who will be responsible to achieve these priority goals and by when?

Developing the Church Profile

- Who were you?
- Who are you now?
- How do you engage culture?
- What is your community context?
- Who do you hope to become?
- What kind of pastor do you need?

Organizational Health

- How would you describe this church's governance style? To what degree are you in alignment with it?

- What are the qualities and behaviors of a healthy board? What needs to change for this church's board to be that kind of board?
- What role will the transitional leader play in facilitating greater organizational health?

The Search Process

- What role will the congregation, board, and denomination play in the search process?
- How will the congregation's pastoral search history affect the present search?
- What denominational resources are available to be used?
- How will we collect and document the information gathered as we prepare a church profile?

Questions to Help Facilitate Group Meetings

At the Beginning

- What do you hope to accomplish in this meeting?
- How will we speak and work with one another?
- What role do you want the facilitator to play in this session?

Checking In

- How are you doing today?
- What has happened since we last met?
- What do you have to report?
- What new information should cause us to shift our focus?

Focus for the Session

- What will the focus of today's meeting be?
- What do we hope to achieve as a result of our meeting?
- How engaged (on scale of 1-10, 1 being low and 10 being high) are you with this topic?

Checking In along the Way

- What's your biggest "aha!" moment or learning so far?
- How do we need to adjust to make sure we get where we want to go?

Taking Action

- What decisions have we made that require further action?
- Who will do what by when?
- What are we saying yes to? What are we saying no to?

Ending the Session

- What are your takeaways?
- What are we committing ourselves to do or be once we leave this meeting?
- When is our next meeting?

Using Tools in Group Coaching and Facilitation

There are a number of tools available that can be used for specific situations. This list is a small sample you can add to.

Group Focus	Tool to Use
Building trust and getting to know each other	Myers-Briggs DISC PSI (Personal Styles Indicator)
Change as a process	The Change Journey "How People Change" worksheet Life Cycle
Conflict and hostility	Iceberg Model
Grief or closure	Grief Cycle History Wall The Change Journey
The strengths we each bring	Strength Finders 2.0
Team Functionality	5 Dysfunctions of a Team by Patrick Lencioni
Planning	Fishbone Dialogue (Root Cause Analysis)
Getting a grip on reality	SWOT Analysis (Strengths, Weaknesses, Opportunities, and Threats)

Table 6: Tools for Group Coaching and Facilitation

Reflective Questions

❖ What is your greatest challenge when facilitating the transitional model?

❖ What are your strengths and weaknesses in the area of facilitation?

❖ What tools would you add to the facilitator's toolbox that you have found useful in working with people?

Appendix A: Key Definitions

Assessment — the process of gathering, collating, and interpreting relevant information for the purpose of informing spiritual discernment and decision-making processes.

Coaching — the ability to listen attentively, ask powerful questions, guide the process of discovering God's agenda, and assist others in bringing God's agenda into reality.

Conflict Management — the process of helping a congregation increase its capacity to value the redemptive aspects of conflict, address past mismanaged conflict, and prepare for future conflicts.

Congregation — a local gathering of Christians (welcoming of non-Christians) which is a visible expression of the church universal and distinguished from other congregations by its unique culture, context, denominational affiliation, and distinctives.

Facilitation — coming alongside a group of people to make their journey, process, or conversation easier by monitoring and balancing the dynamics of relationships, process, and content.

Leadership Board — the official group(s) of people approved by the congregation or authorizing body to be ultimately responsible for the oversight of a congregation. It works in partnership with the pastor(s) and other leaders. Other names used to describe this body include elders, council, lay leaders, synod, official board, and session.

Ministry Planning — the process of reviewing the vision and ministry plan of a congregation with the intention of confirming, adapting, or altering the vision and plan to best meet the challenges of present ministry and kingdom opportunities.

Organizational Health — when congregational systems, infrastructure, and policies have been analyzed and improved so they do a good job of supporting the purpose, values, and vision of a congregation.

Relationship Renewal — the process of repairing, restoring, and improving the relational connection between God and the congregation (upward), the relational connections between the people within the congregation (inward), and the Christian witness of congregational members as they live out their faith with those not yet following Jesus (outward).

Transition — the process of moving from one state or stage to another. For example, a congregation between pastors goes from the stage of "having one particular leader" to a new stage of "having another leader." What happens during that shift is the transition.

Transitional Leader — the person who gives assistance, leadership, and oversight to the intentional interim process. This person is sometimes referred to as the transitional pastor, transitional coach, or intentional interim pastor.

Appendix B: The Denomination's Role

C ongregations in a denominational structure can have a real advantage during a pastoral transition. That is, they *can* – but only if the denomination uses its leadership and influence to encourage healthy and life-giving intentional interim ministry.

Denominational leaders have varying degrees of positional influence. However, when they exercise servant leadership and build trust, they also have *actual influence*. Denominational leaders who desire to encourage an intentional approach to pastoral transitions in congregations under their care might benefit from applying the following five principles. These principles come from observations made while working with numerous denominations.

1. Educate — foster intentional interim ministry language.

It's critical to use a common language to promote the intentional nature of the time between pastors. If the words used to describe interim ministry are outdated, it's time to consider a change. Changing language requires an educational process, but it begins with acknowledging the need for a change. This book could be used to inform the needed discussion on language change.

2. Expedite — respond quickly to a congregation in transition.

Congregations in transition often need outside help sooner rather than later. This depends on the strength and maturity of the congregational leadership. What's important is to determine the needs as quickly as possible so that if outside help is critical, resources can be deployed before it is too late.

A Powerful Lesson from a Lost Opportunity

After leaving the congregation I had served for many years, I watched it lose hope and close its doors in a matter of months. I was shocked and saddened by the loss. I did accept some of the responsibility for the leadership vacuum that developed after I left. I had not built into the congregation a very sustainable leadership community.

What I didn't take responsibility for was the role played by the denominational leaders in how the transition played out. The denomination provided some support but more along the lines of the typical interim approach. There was inadequate assessment of the situation, and a search process was launched immediately, which the congregation was not ready for. The congregation needed healing, closure, stability, pastoral care, and hope. In hindsight, the congregation might have survived had an intentional transitional pastor come alongside early on.

I do believe God worked in spite of what might have been a missed opportunity. I've long since worked this experience through in my heart and mind. I've even been able to support my denomination by equipping and training transitional leaders, and by encouraging a new approach to handling the time between pastors better.

— Cam Taylor

3. Equip — train and support a core of transitional leaders.

Transitional leaders are not just pastors with a different title. They are leaders who have been equipped with both a mindset and a skill set to facilitate an intentional interim. The denomination can play a key role in providing the training dollars, event sponsorship, and ongoing support for those doing this important work.

Training can include on-site workshops, virtual training, coaching, mentoring, networking, and other forms of leadership development. One equipping strategy some denominations are using is setting up a specialized network for their transitional leaders. The same strategy can also be used inter-denominationally.

4. Enfold — utilize qualified transitional leaders from outside.

Effective transitional leaders work well cross-denominationally. They are often in geographical areas where no one from the congregation's own denomination is available. They can also bring some much needed objectivity to an otherwise closed system.

Henry Cloud speaks of the value of the outsider in organizational life in his book *Leadership Boundaries:* "Set a boundary on your tendency to be a 'closed system,' and open yourself to outside inputs that bring you energy and guidance."[75]

5. Empower — provide encouragement and support.

Transitional leadership is a challenging ministry for a variety of reasons. It is short-term, requires a great deal of faith, is very demanding, is geographically diverse, and requires high emotional intelligence.

One way to support transitional leaders is to have a designation for them (similar to those given to chaplains, missionaries, para-church workers, and others). This might open the door to benefits otherwise unavailable. Another way to encourage transitional leaders is to provide a way to connect them with opportunities that match their gifting and skill set.

David Hearn, currently the President of the Christian and Missionary Alliance in Canada, said this while a District Superintendent:

> Our vision is to see every church in our district in pastoral transition contract with an appropriate transitional leader to guide them forward. This vision requires a change in our culture to the point where the value of having a transitional leader is raised to a higher level. I see

transitional leadership as one of the vital ingredients not only in promoting church health but in moving us forward toward a sustainable missional church movement.

Dennis Steele, a Baptist district leader in Western Canada, says this about his role in supporting transitional leaders in local congregations:

Denominational leadership support of the individuals themselves is vital. Different transitional pastors have different skills. Denominational leaders know both churches and their short list of transitional pastors and have an important role in making pairings.

Appendix C: Transition Based on Church Size by Gerry Teichrob

I have served as a transitional ministry specialist with nine congregations, ranging in size from 100 to 1500. How transitional leadership works in each setting differs considerably.

Before discussing the differences, here are some similarities transcending church size:

- All the transitional stages apply to every church of any size.
- It is vital to earn and build trust with the key leadership groups early on in the transition.
- Similar questions arise about the transitional process in churches of all sizes.
- There is typically one group anxious to "get on with it" and find the next pastor as soon as possible while another group is concerned that "we are moving too fast" to thoroughly address key issues needing to be addressed.
- Every church so far, whether large or small, has experienced some attrition both in attendance and finances through the transition.

In addition to similarities, there are significant differences in leading a transition based on church size. [76] Here are four situations I've worked with and the differences I've experienced:

The Solo Pastor Church

The role of the transitional pastor in this setting is, first, to be a pastoral generalist and, second, to be a specialist who does transitional ministry. A high need for the congregation is to know it has a pastor who is present and attending to its needs. The stakeholders are definitely the laity.

Doing the work of transition will be most effective when using a strong pastoral shepherding approach. The relationship between the transitional pastor and the board needs to be carefully analyzed and understood. This relationship is often the reason why the previous pastor left. The strong need for the transitional pastor to be "the pastor" can actually become a hindrance to working through the stages of transition.

The Smaller, Multiple-staff Church

In this context, the transitional pastor works in partnership with an associate and an administrative assistant. The staff can provide a wealth of information to the transitional pastor in the process of getting oriented to the church and can often take on additional pastoral duties so the transitional pastor can focus more energy on the transitional process.

The transitional pastor will need to provide care, guidance, direction, and support to the staff in this setting. The relationship between the staff and board might need careful consideration, as often the lines of accountability and authority are fuzzy.

The Larger, Multiple-staff Church

The larger, multiple-staff church has four to eight staff members and requires the transitional pastor to have staff leadership skills. The departure of the lead pastor often impacts the church staff to the greatest degree in congregations of this size. During the transition, the staff will be able to provide most of the pastoral leadership and care for the ministry of the church.

It has been my approach to avoid doing anything a staff person could do. This allows the ministry leadership load to be shared more equally during the transition. It's easy for the demands of staff leadership to overpower the primary work of addressing the major phases of the transition. The pressure to fill the role left by the exiting lead pastor is quite high.

In a church of this size, there is a great need to effectively address the issues of organizational health and vision clarity since the board and the staff are both empowered and expected to lead. One other factor affecting larger, multiple-staff churches is the looming question of what will happen to the current staff once the new lead pastor is in place. This issue needs special care and attention.

The Mega-church

The mega-church [77] is defined as having eight or more staff members. The transitional pastor in this setting has some unique challenges. The process of being hired as the transitional pastor in a church of this size requires considerable diligence. It is one thing for a church of this size to hire an interim pastor to fill the pulpit and lead the staff. It is quite another for a mega-church to give a transitional pastor the freedom and authority to lead the church through an intentional transition.

My experience has been that my leadership was questioned frequently at each step in the process. I have needed patience and persistence, as I've been asked to continually explain things. This type of church does not tend to see the transitional pastor as a trained specialist as readily as churches smaller in size. There tends to be a greater emphasis on performance.

Understanding the operational values and practices of the church staff and board are critical before proceeding at each stage. The transitional pastor needs a clear understanding of who the key leaders are within the leadership circles and a working understanding of the governance model. A team-based approach to staff leadership and development is essential. The pulpit ministry will require a team approach or the engagement of a well-qualified pulpit voice, supplemented by "strategic preaching events" by the transitional pastor. These "strategic preaching events" address certain aspects of church health for the congregation.

Some General Observations

- The smaller the church, the easier it is to do the overall transitional assessment.
- The larger the church, the more time and effort go into providing stellar communication—in content, frequency, and methodology.
- The larger the church, the less engagement takes place with the congregation. Most of the transitional pastor's time is spent with the staff, the board, and key leadership groups.
- Larger churches tend to struggle more with attrition. They are accustomed to gathering people, as opposed to seeing people depart.
- Financial attrition often impacts the church's ability to sustain the staffing configuration.
- In all kinds of churches, the need for the transitional leader to be an agent of hope is vital.

Gerry Teichrob is the founder and director of Pathways Forward Transitional Ministry Consulting (pathwaysforward.ca). In addition to serving congregations as an experienced transitional pastor, he also provides consulting and coaching for churches in transition and for first-time transitional pastors. He leads the Transitional Pastors' Network for the Pacific District of the Christian and Missionary Alliance in Canada.

Appendix D: Nine Reasons Not to Hire the Transitional Pastor

One question often asked is, "Why can't we just hire the transitional pastor as our next senior pastor?" The thinking goes, "We're comfortable with him (or her) and feel he (she) would make an excellent senior pastor."

Here are nine reasons for not hiring the transitional pastor:

1. The thought can short-circuit closure.

If the possibility exists of hiring the transitional pastor, the closure process may not go deep enough or last long enough. The emotional journey through closure may stop dead in its tracks if the new leader is in view.

2. It might condemn the church to an indefinite period of lamenting.

Pastor and author Dan Reiland puts it this way: "The churches I work with that ignored this stage (closure) often continue to lament for years over the loss of 'the best pastor we ever had.' Or they struggle with anger and distrust for years because the former pastor did not finish well. This is not healthy for the individual, the church or the incoming pastor."[78]

3. It takes away objectivity from the transitional leadership role.

To be effective, transitional pastors need to maintain objectivity in their work. This enables them to deal thoroughly with issues such as conflict, mistrust, and broken relationships. Deep change takes time and works best when led by an outsider with no hidden agendas and nothing to lose.

4. It weakens the leadership of the transitional pastor.

The minute a transitional pastor becomes a candidate for senior pastor, the pastor's leadership is weakened. The pastor may lose the willingness to speak the truth in love because now he or she has something to lose.

5. It prevents deep congregational introspection during the transition.

Transitional ministry is focused on the congregation long before it's focused on the next leader. If the congregation sees the transitional leader as the next pastor, it prematurely takes the focus off the congregation and hinders the work that needs to be done during the transition.

6. Any house-cleaning residue will come with the new pastor into ministry.

If the transitional pastor is called upon to do some house-cleaning, the pastor may carry some of the memory and "residue" of that cleaning. A separate senior pastor will be able to come in without any attachment to that cleaning process and be able to start with a clean slate.

7. The gifts and competencies are different.

Many of the leadership gifts and competencies required for a senior pastor are different from those required for a transitional leader. The best senior pastors do not always make the best transitional leaders, and vice versa.

8. There may be a perceived conflict of interest.

Conflict expert Jim Van Yperen says it this way: "The Intentional Interim cannot and will not be a candidate for any leadership position in the church afterward. This policy is essential so the Intentional Interim can lead with trust, without any real or perceived conflict of interest."[79]

9. The church may be hiring an unintentional interim pastor.

When congregations hire the transitional pastor as the next senior pastor, it often means they have short-circuited the transitional process. They have unfinished business, and they are not ready to commit to a new pastor. As a result, the new pastor may not last long. Research suggests, "If you don't have an intentional interim, you may end up with an unintentional interim."[80]

Appendix E: Outreach Canada and the Story of TLM

The Outreach Canada Team

O utreach Canada is a non-profit organization made up of a diverse group of individuals called to serve Christ in Canada and beyond. The purpose of Outreach Canada is to help facilitate the fulfilling of the Great Commission through the body of Christ. This is done by identifying critical needs and opportunities, championing innovative and appropriate responses, and facilitating cooperative solutions.

Outreach Canada functions as a team of teams working interdependently and synergistically to serve in Canada and around the world. There are four teams making up Outreach Canada:

The Administrative Team — This team cares for finances, human resources, public relations, corporate affairs, information technology, and other administrative tasks. It serves the rest of the team so they can carry out the ministries they are called to do.

The Church in Canada Ministries Team — This team is involved in ministries related to the Canadian church such as church health, conflict mediation, transitional ministry, coaches' training, leadership development, local congregational mission mobilization, the Perspectives course, French language ministry, multicultural ministry, and campus ministry.

The Global Ministries Team — This team focuses on work overseas. The team members are involved in mobilizing and supporting ministry in over a dozen countries in Europe, Africa, Asia, and Latin America.

The Marketplace Ministries Team — This team is involved in missional work within the Canadian marketplace. The team members provide workplace seminars, executive coaching, and corporate chaplaincy in several provinces and with a variety of companies and para-church organizations.

The Story of TLM

Transitional Leadership Ministries (TLM) of Outreach Canada was started in 2003 by Doug Harris. The ministry was birthed out of a realization of the incredible need and opportunity within local congregations for a more intentional approach to the transition between pastors.

Gerry Kraft of Outreach Canada approached Doug Harris about joining Outreach Canada. As they brainstormed and explored where they thought Doug could make the greatest impact, the idea was born to formalize a transitional leadership ministry. Doug's preparation for leading this ministry included many years of ministry experience plus attendance at the transitional ministry course offered by the Interim Ministry Network (IMN).

Once his training was complete, Doug continued serving local congregations as a transitional pastor while at the same time developing TLM. Doug adapted what he had learned from the IMN to the Canadian context. Then, in 2003, he launched Outreach Canada's TLM training course, which has been growing and evolving ever since.

As Doug reflects on where he sees this ministry going, he says, "It is a ministry whose time has come!" He continues to feel excitement and have a passion to see congregations move to a place of strength and greater health during times of transition.

Appendix F: Recommended Resources

Coaching and Facilitation

*Bacon, Terry R., and Karen I. Spear. *Adaptive Coaching: The Art and Practice of a Client-Centered Approach to Performance Improvement*. Palo Alto, CA: Davies-Black Publishing, 2003.

Britton, Jennifer J. *Effective Group Coaching: Tried and Tested Tools and Resources for Optimum Group Coaching Results*. Hoboken, NJ: Wiley, 2010.

*Bens, Ingrid. *Facilitation at a Glance! A Pocket Guide of Tools and Techniques for Effective Meeting Facilitation*. 2nd ed. Salem, NH: Goal/QPC, 2008.

Hall, Chad, Bill Copper, and Kathryn McElveen. *Faith Coaching: A Conversational Approach to Helping Others Move Forward in Faith*. Lenoir, NC: Coach Approach Ministries, 2009.

*Kimsey-House, Henry, Karen Kimsey-House, Phillip Sandahl, and Laura Whitworth. *Co-Active Coaching*. Palo Alto, CA: Davies-Black Publishing, 2007.

Marquardt, Michael. *Leading with Questions: How Leaders Find the Right Solutions by Knowing What to Ask*. Hoboken, NJ: Jossey-Bass, 2005.

Ogne, Steve, and Tim Roehl. *Transformissional Coaching: Empowering Leaders in a Changing Ministry World*. Nashville, TN: B&H Publishing, 2008.

Senge, Peter M., Art Kleiner, Charlotte Roberts, Richard B. Ross, and Ryan J. Smith. *The Fifth Discipline Fieldbook: Strategies and Tools for Building a Learning Organization*. New York: Doubleday, 1994.

Stein, Steven J., and Howard E. Book. *The EQ Edge: Emotional Intelligence and your Success*. Mississauga, ON: Jossey-Bass, 2006.

Stoltzfus, Tony. *Coaching Questions: A Coach's Guide to Powerful Asking Skills*. North Charleston, SC: Booksurge Llc., 2008.

*Stoltzfus, Tony. *Leadership Coaching: The Disciplines, Skills, and Heart of a Christian Coach*. North Charleston, SC: Booksurge Llc., 2005.

Thornton, Christine. *Group and Team Coaching: The Essential Guide*. New York: Routledge, 2010.

*Whitmore, John. *Coaching for Performance: Growing People, Performance and Purpose*. London: Nicholas Brealey Publishing, 2002.

Church Ministry - General

Atkerson, Steve. *Ekklesia: To the Roots of Biblical Church Life*. Atlanta, GA: NTRF, 2003.

Blackaby, Henry T., and Claude V. King. *Experiencing God*. Nashville, TN: B&H Publishing, 1994.

Breen, Mike. *Building a Discipling Culture*. Kindle Edition. Pasadena, CA: 3DM Publishing, 2011.

Campbell, Dennis G. *Congregations as Learning Communities*. Herndon, VA: Alban Institute, 2000.

Kaiser, John Edmund. *Winning on Purpose*. Nashville, TN: Abingdon Press, 2006.

Mann, Alice. *Can Our Church Live?* Herndon, VA: Alban Institute, 1999.

Pickering, Ernest. *For the Hurting Pastor*. Schaumburg, IL: Regular Baptist Press, 1987.

Quick, Kenneth. *Healing the Heart of Your Church*. Saint Charles, IL: Churchsmart Resources, 2003.

Stanley, Andy, and Lane Jones. *Communicating for a Change*. Colorado Springs, CO: Multnomah Books, 2006.

Stevens, R. Paul, and Phil Collins. *The Equipping Pastor*. Herndon, VA: Alban Institute, 2001.

Warren, Rick, ed. *Better Together*. Grand Rapids, MI: Purpose Driven, 2004.

Willard, Dallas. *Renovation of the Heart: Putting on the Character of Christ*. Kindle edition. Colorado Springs, CO: Navpress, 2002.

Conflict and Biblical Peacemaking

Bell, Roy D. *Biblical Models of Handling Conflict*. Vancouver, BC: Regent College Publishing, 1987.

Boers, A. *Never Call Them Jerks*. Herndon, VA: Alban Institute, 1999.

Cloud, H., and J. Townsend. *Boundaries Face to Face*. Grand Rapids, MI: Zondervan, 2003.

Cosgrave, C.H., and D.D. Hatfield. *Church Conflicts: The Hidden Systems Behind the Fights*. Nashville, TN: Abingdon Press, 1994.

Frangipane, F. *It's Time to End Church Splits*. Grand Rapids, MI: Arrow Publications, 2002.

Furlong, Gary T. *The Conflict Resolution Toolbox*. Toronto, ON: John Wiley and Sons Canada, Ltd., 2005.

Greenfield, G. *The Wounded Minister: Healing from and Preventing Attacks*. Grand Rapids, MI: Baker Books, 2001.

*Halverstadt, H.F. *Managing Church Conflict*. Louisville, KY: Westminster John Knox Press, 1991.

Haugk, K. *Antagonist in the Church: How to Identify and Deal with Difficult Conflict*. Minneapolis: Augsburg Publishing House, 1998.

Hopkins, Nancy Myer. *Clergy Sexual Misconduct: A Systems Perspective*. Herndon, VA: The Alban Institute, 1993.

Leas, Speed B. *Discover Your Conflict Management Style*. Herndon, VA: Alban Institute, 1998.

Leas, Speed B. Leadership and Conflict. *Creative Leadership Series*. Edited by Lyle E. Schaller. Nashville, TN: Abingdon Press, 1982.

Leas, Speed B. *Moving Your Church through Conflict*. Bethesda, MD: The Alban Institute, 2002.

Mains, D. *Healing the Dysfunctional Church*. Wheaton, IL: Victor Books, 1997.

Marshall, M. *Beyond Termination: A Spouse's Story*. Nashville, TN: Broadman Press, 1990.

Parrott, L. *High Maintenance Relationships*. Wheaton, IL: Tyndale House, 1996.

Patterson, Kerry, Joseph Grenny, Ron McMillan, and Al Switzler. *Crucial Conversations: Tools for Talking When Stakes Are High*. New York: McGraw-Hill, 2004.

Poirier, Alfred. *The Peace Making Pastor*. Ada, MI: Baker Book House, 2006.

Rediger, G. Lloyd. *Clergy Killers: Guidance for Pastors and Congregations Under Attack*. Louisville, KY: Westminster John Knox Press, 1997.

Rediger, G. Lloyd. *The Toxic Congregation*. Nashville, TN: Abingdon Press, 2006.

Rosenberg, Marshall B. *Nonviolent Communications: A Language of Life.* 2nd ed. Encinitas, CA: Puddledancer Press, 2003.

*Sande, Ken. *The Peacemaker.* North Dartmouth, MA: Baker Books, 1998.

Schrock-Shenk, Ressler. *Making Peace with Conflict.* Scottdale, PA: Herald Press, 1999.

Shelley, Marshall. *Leading Your Church Through Conflict and Reconciliation: 30 Strategies to Transform Your Ministry.* Minneapolis: Bethany House Publishers, 1997.

Shelley, Marshall. *Well-Intentioned Dragons: Ministering to Problem People in the Church.* Minneapolis: Bethany House Publishers, 1995.

Susek, Ron, and James D. Kennedy. *Firestorm: Preventing and Overcoming Church Conflicts.* Ada, MI: Baker Book House, 1999.

*Van Yperen, Jim. *Making Peace: A Guide to Overcoming Church Conflict.* Chicago: Moody Publishers, 2002.

*Van Yperen, Jim. *The Good Confession.* Wheaton, IL: Metanoia Ministries, 2011.

Vennard, J.E. *A Praying Congregation.* Herndon, VA: The Alban Institute, 2005.

Leadership

Anthony, Michael J., and Mick Boersma. *Moving on Moving Forward: A Guide for Pastors in Transition.* Grand Rapids, MI: Zondervan, 2007.

Barton, Ruth Haley. *Strengthening the Soul of Your Leadership: Seeking God in the Crucible of Ministry.* Downers Grove, IL: InterVarsity Press, 2008. Kindle edition.

Boa, Kenneth. *The Perfect Leader: Practicing the Leadership Traits of God.* Eugene, OR: Wipf and Stock Publishers, 2012.

Cloud, Henry. *Boundaries for Leaders: Results, Relationships, and Being Ridiculously in Charge.* New York: Harper Business, 2013.

Friedman, Edwin H. *A Failure of Nerve: Leadership in the Age of the Quick Fix.* Harrisburg, PA: Seabury Books, 2007.

Gilmore, J. *Pastoral Politics: Why Ministers Resign.* New Zealand: AGM Publishers, 2002.

Guinness, Os. *The Call: Finding and Fulfilling the Central Purpose of Your Life.* Nashville, TN: Thomas Nelson, 2003.

Heller, Robert. *Essential Manager: Managing Teams.* New York: DK Adult, 1999.

Hunter, James. *The Servant: A Simple Story About the True Essence of Leadership*. New York: Crown Business, 1998.

Hunter, James. *The World's Most Powerful Leadership Principle: How to Become a Servant Leader*. Colorado Springs, CO: WaterBrook Press, 2004.

Hybels, Bill. *Axiom: Powerful Leadership Proverbs*. Grand Rapids, MI: Zondervan, 2008. Kindle edition.

Kouzes, James M., and Barry Z. Posner, *The Leadership Challenge*. 4th ed. Hoboken, NJ: Jossey-Bass, 2010.

Lencioni, Patrick. *Getting Naked: A Business Fable About Shedding the Three Fears That Sabotage Client Loyalty*. Indianapolis: Jossey-Bass, 2010.

Lencioni, Patrick. *Overcoming the Five Dysfunctions of a Team: A Field Guide for Leaders, Managers, and Facilitators*. Indianapolis: Jossey-Bass, 2005.

*Lencioni, Patrick. *The Five Dysfunctions of a Team: A Leadership Fable*. Indianapolis: Jossey-Bass, 2002.

Lowney, Chris. *Heroic Leadership: Best Practices from a 450-Year-Old Company That Changed the World*. Chicago: Loyola Press, 2003.

Oswald, Roy M. *Clergy Self-Care: Finding a Balance for Effective Ministry*. Herndon, VA: Alban Institute, 1995.

Page, Don. *Servant Empowered Leadership*. Langley, BC: Power to Change Ministries, 2009.

Pappas, Anthony G. *Pastoral Stress: Sources of Tension, Resources for Transformation*. Eugene, OR: Wipf and Stock Publishers, 2005.

Rath, Tom. *Strength Finder 2.0*. New York: Gallup Press, 2007.

Rediger, G. Lloyd. *Fit to be a Pastor: A Call to Physical, Mental and Spiritual Fitness*. Louisville, KY: WJK, 1999.

Sanders, J. Oswald. *Spiritual Leadership*. Chicago: Moody Press, 1967.

Wright, Walter C. *Don't Step on the Rope*. Waynesboro, GA: Paternoster Press, 2005.

Leading Change

Blanchard, Kenneth. *Who Killed Change?* New York: William Morrow, 2009.

Herrington, Jim, Mike Bonem, and James H. Furr. *Leading Congregational Change*. Indianapolis: Jossey-Bass, 2000.

*Heath, Chip, and Dan Heath. *Switch: How to Change When Change is Hard*. New York: Crown Business, 2010.

Kotter, John P. *Leading Change*. Boston: Harvard Business School Press, 1996.

*Kotter, John P., and Dan Cohen. *The Heart of Change*. Boston: Harvard Business School Press, 2002.

Putney, Richard. *Change and Resistance*. Baltimore, MD: Interim Ministry Network, 1992.

*Rendle, Gilbert R. *Leading Change in the Congregation*. Herndon, VA: Alban Institute, 1998.

Search Process

Ketcham, Bunty, and Celia A. Hahn. *So You're on the Search Committee*. Herndon, VA: Alban Institute, 2005.

Kirk, Richard J. *On the Calling and Care of Pastors*. Herndon, VA: Alban Institute, 1984.

Organizational Health

Brown, Jim. *The Imperfect Board Member*. Indianapolis: Jossey-Bass, 2006.

Drucker, Peter F. *The Daily Drucker*. New York: Harper Business, 2009. Kindle edition.

*Engle, Paul E., and Steven B. Cowan. *Who Runs the Church?* Grand Rapids, MI: Zondervan, 2004.

Stahlke, Les. *Governance Matters*. Edmonton, AB: GovernanceMatters.com Inc., 2003.

Weese, Carolyn, and Russell J. Crabtree. *The Elephant in the Boardroom*. Indianapolis: Jossey-Bass, 2004.

Transitional Ministry

*Bridges, William. *Managing Transitions*. New York: Perseus Books, 1991.

*Cloud, Henry. *Necessary Endings: The Employees, Businesses, and Relationships That All of Us Have to Give Up in Order to Move Forward*. New York: Harper Business, 2011.

Gripe, Alan G. *The Interim Pastor's Manual*. Louisville, KY: Geneva Press, 1997.

Hoge, Dean R., and J.E. Wenger. *Pastors in Transition*. Grand Rapids, MI: Wm.B. Eerdmans Publishing, 2005.

Kubler-Ross, Elisabeth. *On Death and Dying*. New York: Scribner, 1997.

Macy, Ralph. *The Interim Pastor*. Herndon, VA: Alban Institute, 1985.

*Manion, Jeff. *The Land Between: Finding God in Difficult Transitions*. Grand Rapids, MI: Zondervan, 2010.

*Mead, Loren B. *A Change of Pastors*. Herndon, VA: Alban Institute, 2005.

Narowitz, Cathleen R. *Worship Resources for the Interim Time*. Baltimore, MD: Ministers-At-Large Program, 1991.

Nicholson, Roger S. *Temporary Shepherds*. Herndon, VA: Alban Institute, 1998.

Vision Clarity & Church Coaching

Avery, William O. *Revitalizing Congregations*. Herndon, VA: Alban Institute, 2002.

Biehl, Bobb. *Masterplanning: The Complete Guide for Building a Strategic Plan for Your Business, Church, or Organization*. Mount Dora, FL: Aylen Publishing, 1997.

Borden, Paul D. *Direct Hit: Aiming Real Leaders at the Mission Field*. Nashville, TN: Abingdon Press, 2006.

Borden, Paul D. *Hit the Bullseye: How Denominations Can Aim Congregations at the Mission Field*. Nashville, TN: Abingdon Press, 2006.

Bullard Jr., George W. *FaithSoaring Churches: A Learning Experience Version*. St. Louis: Lucas Park Books, 2012.

*Bullard Jr., George W. *Pursuing the Full Kingdom Potential of Your Congregation*. Atlanta, GA: Chalice Press, 2005.

*Kraft, Craig C. *New Life in the Church: A Vision Renewal Resource*. Johannesburg: OC Africa, 2008.

Malphurs, Aubrey. *Look Before You Lead: How to Discern and Shape Your Church Culture*. Grand Rapids, MI: Baker Books, 2013.

Miles, David. *ReTURN Resource Kit: Restoring Churches to the Heart of God*. Saint Charles, IL: ChurchSmart Resources, 2005.

Parsons, George, and Speed B. Leas. *Understanding Your Congregation as a System*. Herndon, VA: Alban Institute, 1993.

*Rendle, Gilbert R., and Alice Mann. *Holy Conversations*. Herndon, VA: Alban Institute, 2003.

Schaller, Lyle E. *The Interventionist*. Nashville, TN: Abingdon Press, 1997.

*Steinke, Peter L. *Congregational Leadership in Anxious Times*. Herndon, VA: Alban Institute, 2006.

Steinke, Peter L. *Healthy Congregations: A Systems Approach*. 2nd ed. Herndon, VA: Alban Institute, 2006.

*Steinke, Peter L. *How your Church Family Works: Understanding Congregations as Emotional Systems*. Herndon, VA: Alban Institute, 2006.

*Recommended reading based on the experience of the Transitional Leadership Ministry network

Notes

Introduction

[1] Written by Andrew Hurrell.

Chapter 1

[2] For a thorough explanation of this metaphor, see Chapter 9.

Chapter 3

[3] J. Oswald Sanders, *Spiritual Leadership* (Chicago: Moody Press, 1967), 33.

Chapter 5

[4] *Wikipedia*, s.v. "Conducting," last modified November 26, 2013, http://en.wikipedia.org/wiki/Conducting

Chapter 7

[5] *Collins English Dictionary: Complete and Unabridged*, s.v. "administration," retrieved June 4, 2013, http://www.thefreedictionary.com/administration

[6] Sanders, *Spiritual Leadership*, 202.

Chapter 8

[7] Mike Breen, *Building a Discipling Culture* (Pasadena, CA: 3DM Publishing, 2011), Location 1213, Kindle edition.

[8] The article is available at http://outreachnetwork.ca/Resources.aspx

[9] Ed Stetzer, "Gospel Definitions," *The Exchange* (blog), November 16, 2009, accessed October 15, 2013, http://www.christianitytoday.com/edstetzer/2009/november/gospel-definitions.html

[10] Dallas Willard, *Renovation of the Heart: Putting on the Character of Christ* (Colorado Springs, CO: Navpress, 2002), 238, Kindle edition.

[11] Bob Logan, "The 7 Principles for Incarnational Living," September 5, 2011, accessed November 26, 2013, https://loganleadership.com/2011-09/the-7-principles-of-incarnational-living/

[12] Breen, *Building a Discipling Culture*, Location 1217-1229.

[13] Peter L. Steinke, *How your Church Family Works* (Herndon, VA: Alban Institute, 2006), 4.

[14] Steinke, *How your Church Family Works*, 88-89.

Chapter 9

[15] Used by permission. Copyright 2009 by Rev. George Bullard, DMin. Download a copy at www.BullardJournal.org

[16] Henry T. Blackaby and Claude V. King, *Experiencing God* (Nashville, TN: B&H Publishing, 1994), 32.

[17] George W. Bullard Jr., *Pursuing the Full Kingdom Potential of Your Congregation* (Atlanta, GA: Chalice Press, 2005), 58.

[18] http://www.clergyleadership.com/appreciative-inquiry/appreciative-inquiry-church.cfm

[19] http://www.malphursgroup.com

[20] http://www.thecolumbiapartnership.org/congregationaltransformation.html

[21] http://bobbbiehl.com

[22] http://www.ncd-international.org

[23] http://www.refocusing.org

[24] http://www.sonlife.com

[25] Loren B. Mead, *A Change of Pastors* (Herndon, VA: Alban Institute, 2005), 81.

[26] Gilbert R. Rendle and Alice Mann, *Holy Conversations* (Herndon, VA: Alban Institute, 2003), 103.

[25] Mead, *A Change of Pastors*, 104.

[28] Mead, *A Change of Pastors*, 104.

[29] Mead, *A Change of Pastors*, 105.

Chapter 10

[30] Chris Gambill, "Communication: The Key to All Transition," July 5, 2011, accessed October 15, 2013, http://healthychurch.org/threshold/ communication-key-all-transition

[31] Marcia Hughes, "Emotional Intelligence Backgrounder," accessed November 26, 2013, http://www.cgrowth.com/pressroom.html

[32] For more on Appreciative Inquiry, visit the following website: http://www.clergyleadership.com/appreciative-inquiry/appreciative-inquiry-church.cfm

[33] Doug Harris, as presented during Outreach Canada's TLM training.

Chapter 11

[34] *WordNet 3.0, Farlex clipart collection*, s.v. "engage," retrieved November 6, 2013, http://www.thefreedictionary.com/engage

[35] Aubrey Malphurs, *Look Before You Lead: How to Discern and Shape Your Church Culture* (Grand Rapids, MI: Baker Books, 2013), 83.

Chapter 13

[36] Mead, *A Change of Pastors*, 81.

[37] Mead, *A Change of Pastors*, 81.

[38] Henry Cloud, *Boundaries for Leaders: Results, Relationships, and Being Ridiculously in Charge* (New York: Harper Business, 2013), 199.

Chapter 14

[39] John P. Kotter and Dan Cohen, *The Heart of Change* (Boston: Harvard Business School Press, 2002), 43.

Chapter 15

[40] James Hunter, *The Servant: A Simple Story About the True Essence of Leadership* (New York: Crown Business, 1998), 123.

[41] Chris Lowney, *Heroic Leadership: Best Practices from a 450-Year-Old Company That Changed the World* (Chicago: Loyola Press, 2003), 27.

[42] Lowney, *Heroic Leadership*, 28.

[43] Ruth Haley Barton, *Strengthening the Soul of Your Leadership: Seeking God in the Crucible of Ministry* (Downers Grove, IL: IVP Books, 2012), Location 104-112, Kindle edition.

Chapter 16

[44] James M. Kouzes and Barry Z. Posner, *The Leadership Challenge*, 4th ed. (Hoboken, NJ: Jossey-Bass, 2010), 26.

[45] Stephen R. Covey, *The 7 Habits of Highly Effective People* (New York: Simon and Schuster, 1989), 237-238.

[46] Tony Stoltzfus, *Coaching Questions: A Coach's Guide to Powerful Asking Skills* (North Charleston, SC: Booksurge Llc., 2008), 8.

[47] Chad Hall, Bill Copper, and Kathryn McElveen, *Faith Coaching: A Conversational Approach to Helping Others Move Forward in Faith* (Lenoir, NC: Coach Approach Ministries, 2009), 16.

[48] Peter Senge et al., *The Fifth Discipline Fieldbook: Strategies and Tools for Building a Learning Organization* (New York: Doubleday, 1994), 428.

[49] Ed Stetzer, "Andy Stanley on Communication (Part 1)," *The Exchange* (blog), March 3, 2009, accessed October 1, 2013, http://www.christianitytoday.com/edstetzer/2009/march/andy-stanley-on-communication-part-1.html

Chapter 17

[50] Bill Hybels, *Axiom: Powerful Leadership Proverbs* (Grand Rapids, MI: Zondervan, 2008), Location 1155, Kindle edition.

[51] Glen Blickenstaff, "4 Leadership Styles to Master," February 16, 2012, accessed November 1, 2013, http://www.inc.com/glen-blickenstaff/4-leadership-styles-to-master.html

52 *Wikipedia*, s.v. "Four temperaments," last modified November 13, 2013, accessed July 17, 2013, https://en.wikipedia.org/wiki/Four_temperaments

Chapter 19

53 Os Guinness, *The Call: Finding and Fulfilling the Central Purpose of Your Life* (Nashville, TN: Thomas Nelson, 2003), 29.

54 H.B. London and Neil B. Wiseman, *The Heart of a Great Pastor* (Ventura, CA: Regal Books, 1994), 113.

Chapter 21

55 Walter C. Wright, *Don't Step on the Rope* (Waynesboro, GA: Paternoster Press, 2005), 26.

56 Jim Stovall, "Horse Sense," January 16, 2012, accessed November 14, 2013, http://timmaurer.com/2012/01/16/horse-sense/

57 Stephen M.R. Covey, "Quoteable Quotes," accessed November 14, 2013, http://www.goodreads.com/quotes/255684-the-process-of-building-trust-is-an-interesting-one-but

Chapter 22

58 Bobb Biehl, *Masterplanning,* (Mount Dora, FL: Aylen Publishing, 1997), 18.

59 *Wikipedia*, s.v. "Mind Map," last modified November 13, 2013, http://en.wikipedia.org/wiki/Mind_map

60 Freemind can be downloaded at http://www.edrawsoft.com/freemind.php and Mindjet at www.mindjet.com

61 Biehl, *Masterplanning*, 10.

Chapter 23

62 Peter F. Drucker, *The Daily Drucker* (New York: Harper Business, 2009), 68, Kindle edition.

63 John P. Kotter and Dan Cohen, *The Heart of Change* (Boston: Harvard Business School Press, 2002), 2. See also Kotter's book *Leading Change* and Kotter's stages applied to congregational life in Jim Herrington, Mike Bonem, and James Furr, *Leading Congregational Change* (Hoboken, NJ: Jossey-Bass, 2000).

64 Chip Heath and Dan Heath, *Switch: How to Change When Change is Hard* (New York: Crown Business, 2010), 4.

Chapter 24

65 H.F. Halverstadt, *Managing Church Conflict* (Louisville, KY: Westminster John Knox Press, 1991), 4-5.

66 Ken Sande, *The Peacemaker* (North Dartmouth, MA: Baker Books, 1998), 29.

67 Ressler Schrock-Shenk, *Making Peace with Conflict* (Scottdale, PA: Herald Press, 1999), 23.

68 Justice Institute of BC, *Foundations to Conflict Resolution* (New Westminster, BC: Justice Institute of BC, 2007), 19.

69 Speed B. Leas, "The Levels of Conflict," September 1, 2011, accessed November 21, 2013, http://cntr4conghealth.wordpress.com/2011/09/01/levels-of-conflict-by-speed-leas/

70 Speed B. Leas, *Moving Your Church Through Conflict* (Bethesda, MD: The Alban Institute, 2002), Location 170, Kindle edition.

71 Sande, *The Peacemaker*, 209.

72 Sande, *The Peacemaker*, 209.

Chapter 25

73 Ingrid Bens, *Facilitation at a Glance!* 2nd ed. (Salem, NH: Goal/QPC, 2008), 2.

74 Tom Courry and Ken Mossman, "Behind the Curtain, Creating Magic by Bridging Experiential Training with Coaching." Used with permission.

Appendix B

[75] Cloud, *Boundaries*, 199.

Appendix C

[76] For a summary of church characteristics based on size, see Chapter 3 in Carl F. George's book *Prepare Your Church for the Future* (Tarrytown, NY: Fleming H. Revell, 1991).

[77] In the Canadian context, a mega-church is described as any congregation of 1,000 or more.

Appendix D

[78] Dan Reiland, "Your Church Without A Pastor?" accessed November 26, 2013, http://globalchristiancenter.com/strategy-and-planning/is-your-church-without-a-pastor.html

[79] Jim Van Yperen, "Intentional Interim Pastorate Services," Restoring the Church, accessed November 26, 2013, http://www.restoringthechurch.org/ page/intentional-interim-pastorate-services

[80] Patricia A. Nugent, "The Intentional Interim," *The School Administrator* (April 2011, Number 4, Vol. 68), accessed November 26, 2013, http://www.aasa.org/SchoolAdministratorArticle.aspx?id=18572

Made in the USA
Monee, IL
06 December 2020